Contents

KV-011-965

Introduction

A few months ago the writer had cause to telephone a colleague at home. 'I'll go and get her', said her partner. 'She's computing at the moment – she's very good on the computer.'

Was she writing a new program? No; what the colleague was actually doing was preparing a report and a budget for a new project. She was not, in fact, computing but using the computer as a tool for a work task – a task that did not need the use of a computer but which the computer made easier. It was a task that could have been carried out with pen and paper, writing and arithmetic, and indeed for much of history would have been. When the report and budget were finished she had instructions to email (electronic mail) it to the rest of her team.

This text provides an insight into the concepts of a field of human endeavour known as Information and Communication Technology (ICT), a field that impacts on everybody.

How this text is arranged

The text is in two parts. First, in this Introduction, there is a consideration of what Information and Communication Technology (ICT) is and how it has developed. This is followed by an alphabetical list of key terms and concepts in ICT. At the end of the text is a list of useful websites. Further reading, where appropriate, can be found at the end of the particular concept or definition.

Items within the definitions and concepts that have their own entry are shown in bold with the exception of:

- bits
- bytes
- data
- downloaded
- driver
- email
- file
- hardware
- information
- Information and Communication Technology (ICT)
- Internet
- keyboard

- mouse
- operating system
- software
- Web

as these words appear with considerable frequency. A definition of each, however, is given at the appropriate place in the alphabetical list of concepts and definitions.

What is Information and Communication Technology (ICT)?

ICT is not computing. Computing is the field of study that deals with the design, development and programming of computers. Computers are a vital part of ICT but not the whole part. What the writer's colleague was doing was using the technologies developed by the computer scientists to aid her work. When it was stated that she was 'good on the computer', what was really meant was that she was able to use software applications to facilitate her work tasks and to communicate the results more effectively to her team. Whilst this book contains many computer concepts, it is also concerned with other aspects of ICT such as telephone technologies, satellites and cameras etc. – all part of Information and Communication Technology.

ICT does not only involve computer technologies but is the result of a synergy (defined in the text as the phenomenon where the sum of the parts is greater than the whole) between computer, telephone, camera, radio, television and other technologies so that the results are more than one might expect if one just considered each technology in isolation.

That a computer is powerful especially compared to manual calculating is an accepted fact in today's world. A telephone is now everyday technology. Both computers and telephones have ceased to be wonders and have become part of everyday life. Put them together, however, and the result is eventually the Internet and the World Wide Web, which is in effect a mechanism for linking every computer and the data contained on it to every other computer on the planet. This gives an individual user access to a huge amount of data and a communication network that would have been considered in the realms of science fiction not many years ago. Link the technologies to digital cameras and people can exchange data and see each other in real time with no boundaries of distance. ICT is truly powerful and we are only scratching the surface of what it can do. What was science fiction yesterday is science fact today and (as many who have bought a brand new computer system know only too well) may be approaching obsolescence tomorrow.

This book contains many computing terms and concepts and yet the reader needs to remember that the true power comes from the synergy between the technologies and the networking possibilities they bring with them.

Whilst the term Information and Communication Technology is relatively new, its evolution began when human beings first walked this planet.

All social animals – and humans are a sociable primate – need to communicate, if only to find a mate to ensure the survival of the individual's genes and the species as a whole. Animals that live in groups need to communicate where food is, possible dangers and the nature of the group hierarchy. Gestures and sound are used by many animals but only humans have evolved a specialized verbal and written language.

Humans are not unique in using sound and gestures for communication but the complexity of the language of even the most primitive human society is far, far greater than any other species. There is no doubt that marine mammals of the whale family use sound to communicate in a semi-conversational manner, whilst bees use a visual dance to pass on complex directions to other bees. Humans, however, have developed languages that are both functional and rich in emotional complexities. Human communication is not all verbal, however.

As humans spread over the globe different languages developed. Linguists have traced the roots of many of these languages. As communication has been made easier so components from one language have been adapted into others. Many languages are related to each other. Western European languages often have the roots of their words in Latin. English, the most common international language of communication, has roots in Latin, German and French as well as the original Anglo-Saxon. There are similarities between Spanish and Italian or between the Nordic languages. One of the strangest similarities is that between Hungarian and Finnish, two countries at different extremes of Europe, one on the Danube and the other on the Baltic.

Within languages, dialects develop and with them accents. Whilst many Britons may sound the same to somebody from the USA, Britons can often spot the region of the UK somebody comes from by their accent. Those in the USA can do the same with their accents, New England and Georgia having a quite different sound. Throughout much of the twentieth century there was a tendency in the UK to try to eliminate regional variation and have everybody speaking what is termed 'received pronunciation' (the Queen's or BBC English). This trend has passed and regional dialects are welcomed because they add variety. There have also been attempts recently, especially within Europe, to revive ancient languages such as Welsh, Gaelic, Breton, Catalan etc. Many of these were repressed for political reasons in order to bring their speakers into the mainstream of the larger nation. There is now a realization that language variation does not always imply separatism.

In the US there are a number of languages spoken. Whilst English is the most widely used there are a large number of Spanish speakers together with Chinese, Yiddish and the Native American languages. Countries such as India that have a large number of indigenous languages often adopt an official language for trade and business purposes – in the case of India it is English.

The oldest language preserved in writing, Sumerian, was written in cuneiform script. Its earliest records date from about 3000 BC; after about 2000 BC it was no longer spoken, but it continued in use as a literary language until cuneiform writing died out in about the first century BC. Whilst much of the world uses a Roman-style script, Asian languages and Arabic use symbols whilst Cyrillic script is common in countries with a Slavonic background. The natural eye movements of a baby are from right to left – the way Arabic and many other Asian languages are written. Users of languages such as English that run left to right have to train their eyes to do this.

In addition to verbal and written language there is a whole sub-area of study, that of non-verbal communication. The importance of understanding body language cannot be overestimated. Body language is a lower-level communication method than spoken or written language and whilst not as subtle does indicate true feelings. If somebody says, 'I'm pleased to see you' but the body language indicates otherwise, it is the latter that is likely to indicate the person's true feelings.

Up to 1830 the fastest that a normal person could send a message to somebody else was about 15 m.p.h. – the speed of a horse. By 1829, the locomotives of the Liverpool and Manchester Railway could achieve double that and by 1904 the Great Western Railway locomotive *City of Truro* had achieved 100 m.p.h. The development of railways produced a need to communicate for signalling purposes and this led to the development of, firstly, the electric telegraph, then the telephone and later wireless (radio) communications. These operated at the speed of light; thus in a very few years communication speeds increased from a few miles per hour to many thousands of miles per second.

Incidentally, the increase in speed brought about by the development of railways led to the introduction of a standard time throughout the UK. When people only moved at the speed of a horse the time differences caused by using local time (i.e., setting noon as the time when the sun was directly overhead at each individual location) caused no problems. As the speed of transport increased it became necessary, for obvious reasons, to keep the same time at both ends of a railway line and so 'Railway Time' was adopted where noon was defined as the time the sun was overhead at the Greenwich meridian, this soon becoming known as Greenwich Mean Time – GMT. A physical means of communicating people and artefacts brought about a change in the way we recorded time.

You can read more about language, communication and its development in:

Buckley, B. (2003), *Children's Communication Skills from Birth to Five Years* (Routledge).
Stanton, N. (2003), *Mastering Communication* (Basingstoke: Palgrave Macmillan).

A brief history of computing

It can be argued that ancient edifices such as the Pyramids and Stonehenge are in fact the earliest known computers. If the theories that they were used for astrological and astronomical study are correct then they may have been the ancestors of the computer on your desk today. It seems clear to many researchers that the structures aided ancient astronomers and astrologers in predicting the position of planets, perhaps for the timing of religious festivals. One thing they shared in common with the first generation of electrical-mechanical and electronic computers was that they were not portable.

The first portable calculating machine was the abacus, a technology still in use in the Far East today. When the beads are moved around, according to programming rules memorized by the user, all regular arithmetic problems can be performed, and very quickly too, as those who have seen an abacus used by an expert can testify. This is something that the expert abacus user shares with those proficient with a slide rule.

Blaise Pascal in France is credited with building the first digital computer, in 1642. His machine added numbers entered using dials and was made to help his father who was a tax collector. No doubt Mr Pascal Snr would be amused, if he was here today, to find that tax returns can now be submitted via a computer and the Internet! In 1671, Gottfried Wilhelm von Leibniz invented a computer that could, initially, only perform addition. Multiplication is only repeated addition and von Leibniz soon added a multiplication function. In the 1960s similar machines were still in use in UK schools.

In 1812 Charles Babbage based in Cambridge (UK), realized that many long calculations, especially those needed to make mathematical tables, were really a series of predictable actions that were constantly repeated. He set out to find a means of doing this automatically. He began to design an automatic mechanical calculating machine, which he called a difference engine, and by 1822 he had built a working model. With financial help from the British government, Babbage started fabrication of a full-size machine. It was intended to be steam-powered and fully automatic, including the printing of the resulting tables, and commanded by a fixed instruction program. Needless to say, it was somewhat beyond the available technologies of the time. Steam power was relatively new and it is not surprising that Babbage wished to use the new power of the age. His friend Isambard Kingdom Brunel, as inventive as Babbage, was doing that with his railways and steamships. Brunel was so impressed with Babbage that he provided him with his own special train – a singular honour indeed.

The difference engine, although having limited adaptability and applicability, was a great advance. Babbage continued to work on it until 1833 when he began to develop a general-purpose, fully program-controlled, automatic mechanical digital computer. Babbage called this idea an analytical engine. The plans for this engine required a decimal computer operating on numbers of 50 decimal digits (or words) and having a storage capacity (memory) of 1000 such digits. The built-in operations were supposed to include everything that a modern general-purpose computer would need, even the all-important Conditional Control Transfer Capability that would allow commands to be executed in any order, not just the order in which they were programmed.

The analytical engine was designed to use punched cards (similar to those used in the Jacquard looms of the time and which had allowed the mass production of identical designs of woven fabrics), which would be read into the machine from reading stations. Punched cards remained an important part of computing well into the 1970s. The machine was supposed to operate automatically, by steam power, and require only one operator to monitor it. Unfortunately these wonderful ideas never reached fruition and whilst his friend Brunel was voted as the second greatest Briton ever (after Winston Spencer Churchill), Babbage remains unknown to the majority of people. Various reasons are given for his failure. The most commonly stated explanation is the lack of precision machining techniques at the time. Another suggestion is that Babbage was working on the solution of a problem that few people in 1840 really needed to solve. After Babbage there was a temporary loss of interest in automatic digital computers.

Between 1850 and 1900 great advances were made in mathematical physics, and it came to be understood that most events occurring in nature can be measured or described by one differential equation or another, so that any easy means for their calculation would be helpful. Moreover, from a practical view, the availability of steam power caused manufacturing (boilers), transportation (steam engines and boats) and commerce to prosper and led to a period of many engineering achievements. The designing of railways and the making of steamships, textile mills and bridges required differential calculus to determine such things as:

- centre of gravity;
- centre of buoyancy;
- moment of inertia;
- stress distributions;
- flow patterns of hull through water;
- strength calculations;
- power-to-weight calculations;

and to provide the precision required for fast-moving components. Precision and accuracy became more important than they had ever been.

Even the assessment of the power output of a steam engine needed mathematical integration. A strong need thus developed for a machine that could rapidly perform many repetitive calculations. The range of improvements included:

- accumulation of partial results;
- storage and automatic re-entry of past results (a memory function);
- printing of the results.

Each of these required manual installation. These improvements were mainly made for commercial users, and not for the needs of science.

A whole new educational system began to be developed, that of technical education. The engineers of the time needed training not only in design and construction but also in mathematics and the use of such tools as logarithms and slide rules. Not many years ago one could still find those who preferred a mechanical slide rule to the use of a computer – such had been their training.

By the 1890s devices had been developed that could read the information that had been punched into the cards automatically. This ability reduced reading errors dramatically, increased work flow and, most importantly, stacks of punched cards could be used as easily accessible memory of almost unlimited size save that of storage. Furthermore, different problems could be stored on different stacks of cards and accessed when needed.

These advantages were seen by commercial companies and soon led to the development of improved punch-card-using computers created by the now well-known names of International Business Machines (IBM), Remington Burroughs, and other corporations. These computers used electromechanical devices in which electrical power provided mechanical motion. Compared with modern computers, these machines were slow, usually processing 50–220 cards per minute, each card holding about 80 decimal numbers (characters). At the time, however, punched cards were a huge step forward. They provided a means of input/output, and memory storage on a huge scale. For more than 50 years after their first use, punched-card machines did most of the world's first business computing, and a considerable amount of the computing work in science.

The introduction of what we recognize today as computers can be traced back to the 'Harvard Mk I' and Colossus, both developed in 1943 during the Second World War. Colossus was an electronic computer built at the British government code-breaking centre at Bletchley Park in Britain and was designed specifically to break the codes used by the German armed forces. The cracking of such codes by Alan Turing and his colleagues – Enigma being one of the most important – has been the subject of various fiction and non-fiction texts. The 'Harvard Mk I' was a more general-purpose electromechanical programmable computer built at Harvard University with backing from International Business Machines (IBM). These computers were among the earliest of what are now known as first-generation computers. Turing also carried out the first work into what is now known as **artificial intelligence** (AI) during his time at Bletchley park. Many of the important industrial and military developments of the immediate pre-war and wartime periods needed huge amounts of calculating power: code breaking, radar, sonar etc. were as much scientific as military successes. The Polaris nuclear missile system, nuclear energy and the space race all became reliant on huge increases in calculating power.

First-generation computers were normally based around wired circuits containing vacuum tubes (commonly referred to as valves) and used punched cards as the main (non-volatile, i.e., data is not lost when the power is switched off) storage medium. Another general-purpose computer of this era was 'ENIAC' (Electronic Numerical Integrator and Computer) which was completed in 1946. It was typical of first-generation computers, weighing over 30 tonnes and needing 18,000 electronic valves that consumed around 25 kW of electrical power. It was, however, capable of 100,000 calculations a second – an unbelievable amount of calculating power for those days. Similar thermionic valve technology was to be found in the radios and early television receivers of the 1950s and 1960s.

The invention of the transistor in 1947 led to computers becoming smaller as transistors replaced the inefficient valves with a much smaller and more reliable component. As transistors became more efficient in the late 1950s they also revolutionized the home entertainment market with the development of portable radios and more efficient television receivers at relatively affordable prices. Transistorized computers are normally referred to as 'second generation' and dominated the late 1950s and early 1960s. Despite using transistors and printed circuits, these computers were still bulky and strictly the domain of universities and governments. UNIVAC at Manchester University took up considerable space and yet would be totally outperformed by any of today's laptops.

The Cold War provided a huge impetus to computer development. The advances in missile and space technology, especially that of submarine-launched ballistic missiles (SLBM), Polaris and later Trident in the US and UK required huge increases in calculating ability, as mentioned above. These were huge scientific and manufacturing programmes. Not only had calculations to be made but scientists across continents needed to be in contact with each other to exchange data – the birth of the Internet was being witnessed (see below).

Jack St Claire Kilby's invention of the integrated circuit, or microchip, in 1958 led to even greater miniaturization and increases in performance both for large computers and also for the development of smaller business-oriented machines. The computer was moving out of academia and into the world of business and was soon to move into the lucrative domestic market.

On 15 November 1971, Intel released the world's first commercial microprocessor, the 4004. Fourth-generation computers were then developed, using a microprocessor to locate much of the computer's processing abilities on a single (small) chip. Coupled with one of Intel's major inventions – the RAM chip (kilobits of memory on a single chip) – the microprocessor allowed fourth-generation computers to be even smaller and faster than ever before. The microprocessor also allowed the development of microcomputers, personal computers that were small and cheap enough to be available to ordinary people. The first such personal computer was the MITS Altair 8800, released at the end of 1974, but it was followed by computers such as the Apple I and II, Commodore PET and eventually the original IBM PC in 1981. The microcomputer has become known generically as a PC (personal computer) but this was originally an IBM brand name. PCs took the use of computers out of the purely business, scientific and academic arenas and into the domestic environment.

In the mid-1880s the UK government was in the process of implementing its first computers for primary school programmes. The three choices were a Research Machines (RML) 480Z, a metal-cased, robust machine, a BBC Model B or a Sinclair Spectrum. None of the three had a hard disk, all programs being loaded via cassette recorder. Primitive as they were, they provided hands-on computer experience for a generation that was to grow up with the computer as a part of daily life.

Many of the early home computers were initially used for games, with many early examples, such as those produced by Atari, being pure games platforms (a genre still present in Playstation etc.). However, users soon found domestic applications, especially word processing, spreadsheets, graphics and desktop publishing that gained rapidly in popularity.

Although processing power and storage capacities have increased beyond all recognition since the 1970s the underlying technology of LSI (large-scale integration) or VLSI (very-large scale integration) microchips has remained basically the same, so that most of today's computers are widely regarded as still belonging to the fourth generation. By 2000 there were few offices across the world and few homes in the developed world that did not contain a PC in some form or another. Most vehicles and many domestic appliances had embedded computers. The future will see smaller and smaller yet more powerful computers, perhaps using biological means of memory. The growth in computing has been almost exponential, a growth that seems set to continue.

Although computers are now very sophisticated the basic concept has not changed and can be illustrated as shown in Figure 1. The input method may be:

- keyboard
- mouse
- trackerball
- graphics tablet
- touchscreen
- from memory
- scanner
- email
- the Internet
- audio device for music

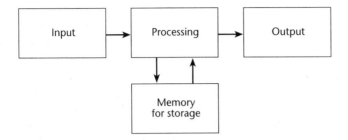

Figure 1   Basic computer model

- video device
- microphone

Outputs are:

- screen
- to memory
- printer
- email
- facsimile (fax)
- plotter
- external drive
- web camera
- speakers

The processor takes data from the input and acts upon it to produce information in the form of a meaningful output.

The Internet

The Internet began with the linking together of a series of computers in the US DARPA (Defense Agency Research Projects Administration) to form what became known in 1969 as ARPAnet, and was designed to protect military communications in the event of a nuclear attack – a very real fear in the political climate of the time. The system used three university hosts in California and one in Utah. Later in the 1970s the US academic community set up a purely civilian network funded by the NSF (National Science Foundation), which linked an increasing number of US and foreign universities via NSFnet. For the first time academics and researchers could communicate text via a new medium, electronic mail (email).

As students who had used email began to take up positions within the private sector it was not long before large commercial organizations in the USA, beginning with the computer companies such as IBM and Hewlett-Packard, began to use email as a business communications tool by linking their systems to the NSFnet.

In 1993 Marc Andreessen and his colleagues at the University of Illinois introduced the first web browser software (Mosaic), a software application for the UNIX operating system, which was later adapted for both the Apple Macintosh and Microsoft Windows® operating systems. As more and more computers became linked, ISP (Internet Service Provider) companies were founded so that by the middle of the 1990s organizations in both the public and private sectors were not only using email but were beginning to design and post web pages. The WWW (World Wide Web) had been born. The Web's actual data and place of birth was CERN (the European Organization for Nuclear Research) in 1990.

A note on storage size and speed

- The prefix 'kilo' (for example, kB and kHz – kilobyte and kilohertz) stands for 1000 (1 kB is actually 1024 bytes)

- The prefix 'mega' (for example, MB and MHz – megabyte and megahertz) stands for 1,000,000

- The prefix 'giga' (for example, GB and GHz – gigabyte and gigahertz) stands for 1000,000,000

The storage capacity of a disk etc. is measured in bytes (see main definitions). The speed of a computer is measured in Hertz after the physicist of that name – 1 Hz = 1 cycle per second.

A typical home-use PC may have a speed of 1.6 GHz and a hard disk capacity of 40 GB. The higher the speed, the faster the computer can process data and the greater the capacity, the more data that can be stored. The story of computing has been that of a continuous increase in speed, capacity and connectivity.

Case study: e-commerce and Amazon.com

One of the earliest e-commerce success stories was that of Amazon, the Internet book, music, software and latterly electronics retailer, as shown below (adapted from the author's *Mastering the Globalization of Business*, published by Palgrave Macmillan in 2004). Globally, Amazon.com is probably one of the best-known names of the new dot.com companies that seemed to have sprung up (and sometimes disappeared just as quickly) at the end of the 1990s and into the early years of the new century. Amazon has revolutionized firstly book sales, then software and music sales in the USA, the UK, Germany, Canada, France and Japan.

The founder of Amazon.com is ex-Princeton graduate Jeff Bezos, the son of a Cuban immigrant to the USA. After graduating from Princeton, Bezos became involved with the computer side of the banking industry and began to see the potential of the Internet for commerce. It is now generally agreed that the birth of the World Wide Web was in 1993, but even before that a number of proactive entrepreneurs were registering website names. Amongst them were a very small number of booksellers, the first being Computer Literacy. Research that Bezos carried out for his then employer in 1994 showed that Internet usage was growing at the time at an incredible 2300 per cent per annum. Bezos considered exactly which products/services would be best to offer using the Internet as the supplier–customer interface. His choices included software, clothing and books. His research indicated that books, a product going back centuries, were a very good choice for retailing through the most up-to-date medium of trade.

The book trade has always been fragmentary, with a large number of publishers in different countries together with retail outlets ranging from small, independent one-site operations to national and latterly international chains. In the USA even the largest of the publishers, Random House, had less than 10 per cent of the market, and the two largest retail chains, Barnes and Noble and Borders (who also have a large UK operation) accounted for less than 25 per cent of the $30 billion of adult US book sales in 1994. Since then children's book sales have grown considerably, fuelled by the Harry Potter phenomenon. Despite its fragmentation, however, book selling is big business because reading is a popular activity – in 1996 global book sales netted $82 billion. In the UK the 1990s saw a deregulation within the industry with the scrapping of the Net Book Agreement that had fixed prices. Booksellers could now discount and the major chains did just that, '3 for 2' deals etc. on novels becoming increasingly common. In the USA this trend had been led by Crown Books in the 1980s.

The major problem that traditional bookstores have is the need for space for selling and warehousing. Even the largest store in the USA or UK could only carry a small percentage of the 1.5 million English-language books in print at any one time and thus many books had to be ordered, thereby forcing the customer to wait. Waiting for a novel is one thing; waiting for a book needed for study or business can be a major issue. Bezos realized that a virtual bookstore using the Internet would mean an unlimited number of titles available to the customer. His operation could acquire stock direct from the publishers or from one of the small number of book distributors. The Internet technology would make the customer's task of searching for a title relatively simple and a check could be kept on customer preferences so that recommendations could be made, thus personalizing the service to the same level as is possible when using a small independent book-store on a regular basis. There, it is the owner who knows the customer; in the Bezos vision it is the computer. The key issue would be that of speedy delivery of the book to the customer.

Moving to Seattle, Bezos spent much of 1994 meeting people and learning about the book business. He conducted a thorough analysis of the market and the competition, and, in November 1994, Bezos and his associates began the Amazon.com operation in a converted garage in a section of Seattle. It used the database of 'books in print' and information from the Library of Congress (look at the front of nearly any book in the English language that is likely to reach the US or UK markets and you will find Library of Congress and the British Library statements that the book is included in their catalogues). The company was launched to the public in 1995, by which time it had acquired a database of more than one million titles. An ordering system, customer identification system, distribution, and the all-important credit card facilities had been established. No longer need those with access to the Internet (a growing percentage of the US population) travel to a bookstore. No matter how remote they were, they could browse the book lists online and order with confidence. The only thing they could not do was scan the shelves and the pages of the books on them. However, more and more information about content is available in the media, on the Internet and on the Amazon.com site itself, so that virtual browsing has become more of a reality.

From the beginning, Amazon.com discounted their bestsellers by 10 per cent, with some titles discounted by up to 30 per cent. The way the site works means that it provides a degree of a personal relationship and that entering the site (provided the 'cookie' has not been deleted from the PC) elicits a personal welcome back and news of the latest releases in the customer's particular areas of interest based on previous purchasing patterns.

Like the vast majority of the early dot.com operations Bezos lost money – $303,000 in 1995. However, even early on in the history of the company over 2000 people per day were visiting the site and within two years this would increase to 80,000. By 1996 Bezos had acquired sufficient venture capital to expand the Amazon.com operation and the company had increased to 150 employees and, more importantly, $16 million in sales – prompting an approach from the major bookseller Barnes and Noble, although no deal materialized. Also in that year an associates programme was launched whereby the owners of other websites could direct their visitors to Amazon.com and receive a small payment if this resulted in a purchase.

In 1997, Amazon.com made its IPO (initial public offering). Despite the fact that the company was still losing money (£3 million in the first quarter of 1997), sales had boomed and investors considered Amazon.com worth buying, with the result that the IPO was oversubscribed. The opening price was $18 and after an initial rise and fall ended the year at $52 – not bad for a company that had only made losses.

Amazon's global expansion began in 1998 when Bezos commenced talks with Bertelsmann AG, the Germany media giant that already had a small Internet bookselling operation, BOL. This led to nothing but Bertelsmann later acquired 50 per cent of the Barnes and Noble online operation – competition was growing. Amazon then acquired a UK online operation and a smaller on-line bookshop in Germany. This gave Bezos an entry into the lucrative UK and German markets. The UK was important, as London is a large publishing centre for English-language books. Most of the major publishers operate parallel UK and US operations, publishing simultaneously in both countries. With further expansion into Canada it can be seen that, with the exception of Germany, Bezos was moving into the global market for English-language books – the biggest of the world's markets. Many of the textbooks used in Africa and India are in English. These moves led to the formation of Amazon.co.uk in the UK and Amazon.co.de in Germany. Amazon customizes its sites for national preferences. A small example of this is that the customer loads their purchases onto a shopping cart on Amazon.com but into a shopping basket on Amazon.co.uk (Americans and Canadians use shopping carts in supermarkets whilst the British refer to a shopping trolley). On the UK site US-published and -supplied books are priced in both dollars and pounds sterling.

This expansion has led to certain copyright problems. US copyright law bars the importation of copyrighted books for commercial resale (but not for private use). Bezos considered that a US citizen buying on-line from Amazon.co.uk (easily accessed from the USA) was doing the same as flying to London, buying the book and bringing it back to the USA. This argument is still underway. Certainly users of Amazon.co.uk have no difficulty in acquiring US books through the site, as the writer can testify. The decision to expand into the UK and Germany was sensible as much of the British Commonwealth will happily buy from the UK and central Europeans are accustomed to doing business with German companies. With their local distribution systems, Amazon.co.uk and its German counterpart have grown rapidly to become an established part of the local book-buying scene.

By 1999, Amazon as a group had expanded into CD and DVD sales through its online Zshops and in 2001 started to sell electronic items including cameras. In 1999 total sales were $2.6 billion. Also in 2001 Amazon acquired the Borders online operation. By 2001 the global expansion had included two further very important markets – France and Japan.

In addition to the associates' programme, where writers can link their websites directly to Amazon, the company has also begun to offer second-hand sales using both dedicated booksellers and private individuals. Amazon takes care of the payments and the seller agrees to despatch the material within one or two working days. From books it was a natural expansion, beginning in 1999, into music and then software. The next move was into software delivery although using physical delivery rather than on-line; and then into electronic products, digital cameras etc. The UK began to offer this service in April 2003 with Canada, Germany and Japan following over a period of just a few months.

One of the recent successes of publishing are the Harry Potter books, which have made the Scottish author J. K. Rowling a multimillionaire. Children have queued for hours waiting for bookstores to open at midnight in order to obtain the latest instalment of the boy wizard's adventures. Advance sales have been the highest ever recorded. In January 2003 *Harry Potter and the Order of the Phoenix* became the number 1 Amazon bestseller months before it was actually launched in June 2003. It was one of the first English-language books to make the French number 1 spot. Amazon teamed up with the distribution giant Federal Express (FedEx) and the United States' Postal Service to deliver no less than a quarter of a million copies to US homes on the same day the book was available in bookshops. This was a massive undertaking.

There is no doubt that despite the problems of the dot.com companies and the time it takes to move into profit, Bezos has provided the world with an effective means of buying an old product – the humble book is as important today as it has been throughout history for the transmission of knowledge, culture and ideas and for providing sheer pleasure through reading. Amazon has used ICT to move into new global markets, adapting its local website to meet the needs of the local customers.

Accelerator

An accelerator is a device or program designed to improve the speed of a hardware peripheral or software program. An example of an accelerator would be a graphics or 3D accelerator. A graphics accelerator is a hardware peripheral that contains its own processor and **RAM** enabling the card to perform at accelerated speeds without decreasing the performance of the computer. Other examples of accelerators are various utilities used to increase the performance of hardware devices, for example, download accelerators used to help increase the speed of **download** times on computer **modems**.

Acceptable Use Policy (AUP)

An AUP (Acceptable Use Policy) is an agreement made between a user and another party on what a service can and cannot be used for. By utilizing the service the user is agreeing to the terms in the policy. Externally this type of agreement may be made between a user and an Internet Service Provider (ISP) and forms part of the legal contract between the user and the **ISP**. Many organizations have an acceptable use policy on what employees can and cannot use computers for. Personal emails may be forbidden, as may accessing non-work-related sites on the Internet. Serious breaches such as downloading inappropriate or pornographic material may result in instant dismissal. *See also* **misuse of organizational ICT**.

Acoustic coupler

Included as a matter of historical interest, the acoustic coupler was a device that became popular in the 1970s which allows a computer to connect to other computers. The first acoustic couplers connected to the telephone handset and transmitted at a speed of 300 **baud** as **analogue** sound signals that were transferred to digital by the acoustic coupler. The phone handset actually sat in a cradle attached to the coupler. Although this technology seems very basic today, in the 1970s it allowed computers on different sites to transfer data. Today users who wish to transmit data over phone lines commonly use a **modem** to connect to other computers or networks instead of the acoustic coupler because of the dependability, speed and ease of use.

ACPI (Advanced Configuration and Power Interface)

ACPI provides a flexible and abstract hardware interface standard that provides a standard way to integrate power management features throughout a PC system, including hardware, operating system and application software. This enables the system to automatically turn **peripherals** on and off, such as **CD-ROMs**, **network cards**, **hard disk drives** and **printers**, as well as consumer devices connected to the PC such as VCRs, televisions, telephones and stereos. With this technology, peripherals can also activate the PC. For example, inserting a disk into a linked stand-alone **DVD** player can turn on the PC, which could then activate a large-screen television and high-fidelity sound system. It is this type of **ICT** development that is leading to integrated ICT systems within the home where all components are linked and can interact in addition to their stand-alone functions.

ACPI is the foundation for the OnNow industry initiative that allows system manufacturers to deliver computers that will start at the touch of a key on the **keyboard**. ACPI design is essential to take full advantage of power management and **Plug and Play**.

Active window

The current window that is in front of all the other windows and is currently being used on a Graphical User Interface (**GUI**). See Figure 2.

A

ActiveX

ActiveX controls are software modules based on Microsoft's Component Object Model (COM) architecture. They add functionality to software applications by seamlessly incorporating pre-made modules with the basic software package. Modules can be interchanged but still appear as parts of the original software.

On the Internet, ActiveX controls can be linked to web pages and downloaded by an ActiveX-compliant browser. ActiveX controls turn web pages into software pages that perform like any other program launched from a **server**.

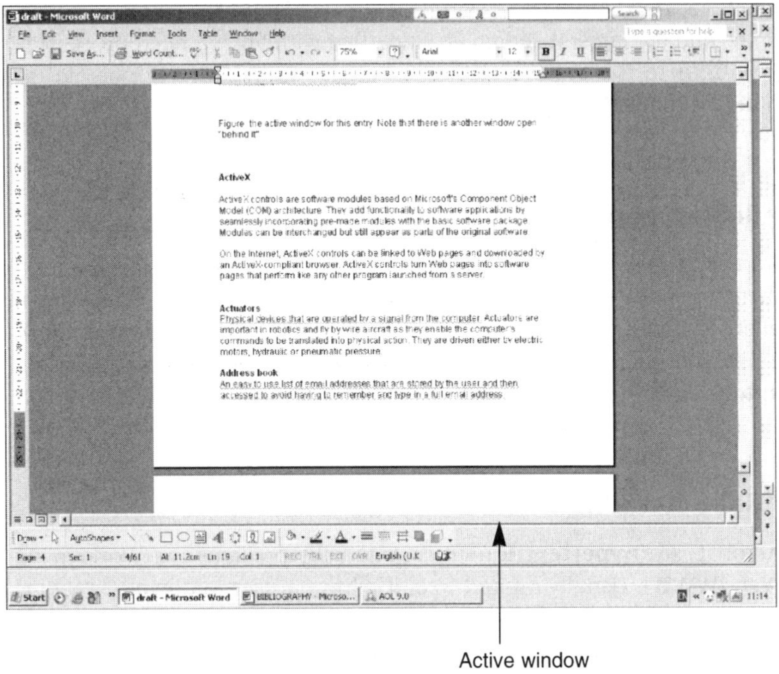

Active window

Figure 2   The active window for this entry (note that there is another window open 'behind it')

Actuators

Physical devices that are operated by a signal from the computer. Actuators are important in robotics and fly-by-wire aircraft as they enable the computer's commands to be translated into physical action. They are driven either by electric motors, or by hydraulic or pneumatic pressure. Any piece of equipment that has physical motion controlled by a computer requires actuators. Aircraft (as mentioned above) contain a large number of actuators. The size of the control surfaces on a modern airliner is such that a human being could not move them all and requires the use of actuators to assist. In the latest aircraft the pilot operates a control (either a traditional control column or a joystick) linked to the aircraft's computer systems and it is these systems that operate the actuators. Computer Aided Manufacture (**CAM**) uses actuators to operate

A

machine tools. Medical researchers use actuators to operate artificial limbs and the latest research is concerned with linking microprocessors (*see* CPU) to the brain and then to actuators in order to operate 'as nature intended'.

Address book

An easy-to-use list of email addresses that are stored by the user and then accessed to avoid having to remember and type in a full email address. Email programs can be set to accept only messages from those in the address book if the user so wishes. This is one means of avoiding **spam**.

Adobe Acrobat

Acrobat is a **hypertext** format that actually predates the World Wide Web (**WWW**). Usually offered free, it allows a user to download multi-page forms as a single Portable Document Format (**.pdf**) and is not dependent on a particular operating system. If the user does not possess Acrobat, the vast majority of companies etc. that have their forms in Acrobat format will offer the facility to download Acrobat from their site for free. Acrobat provides a means for forms to be printed in exactly the same format as they appear on the website. It is also used to download timetables as these require to be in exactly the same format as on the web page.

See also **PDF (Portable Document Format)**.

ADSL (Asynchronous Digital Subscriber Line)

ADSL provides a huge increase in access speed for **networks** over traditional telephone-line-based **modems**. ADSL is the technical term for what is commonly referred to as 'Broadband' and provides for increases in download speeds by a factor of 10–20 over a normal **telephone** line. **Broadband** requires specially equipped telephone exchanges, a process that is on-going in the UK. ADSL is superseding ISDN. Broadband connections are typically 256 kilobytes per second (kBps) or faster.

Adware

Adware may also be called **malware, sneakware** or **spyware**. These are all types of software program that are installed on a computer without a user's consent or knowledge while another program is being installed on the computer. These programs are used to track an individual's Internet activities and/or habits to help companies to target their advertising more efficiently.

These types of programs can be easily located and removed from a computer using software utilities available on the Internet.

Algorithm

An algorithm is a sequence of steps needed to solve logical or mathematical problems. Certain cryptographic algorithms are used to **encrypt** or decrypt data files and messages and to sign documents digitally.

Allocation unit

The smallest amount of disk space that can be allocated to hold a file. For Microsoft Windows® all file systems are organized on the **hard disk** based on allocation units. The smaller the allocation unit size, the more efficiently a disk stores information. If no allocation unit size is specified when formatting the disk, Windows® picks default sizes based on the size of the volume. These default sizes are selected to reduce the amount of space that is lost and the amount of fragmentation (see under **defragmentation**) on the volume. An allocation unit is also called a cluster.

Alphanumeric

Description of text or the availability of both numbers and letters. For example, John2792Jones is a short **string** of alphanumeric characters. Alphanumeric is commonly used to help describe the availability of text that can be entered or used in a field such as a **password**.

A

ALU (Arithmetic Logic Unit)

A component of the Central Processing Unit (**CPU**) that is used for logical comparisons of data and for arithmetic operations. By their nature computers are extremely efficient at processing numbers and this was their original use.

Analogue

Analogue refers to the process of using physical variables, for example voltage or light intensity, to denote a numeric value. Analogue signals vary across a wide range whereas digital signals possess only two states, on/off, yes/no, 1/0 etc. An analogue watch has hands that move around the dial whereas a **digital** watch uses only discrete numbers.

Analogue–digital converter

A device that converts an **analogue** signal into a **digital** form for reading by a computer. The intensity of a light source (an analogue) measure can be digitalized and then read by a computer. The 'fly by wire' systems on modern jet aircraft make considerable use of devices that convert analogue signals to digital and vice versa. The transducers that detect movement attached to the control column send analogue signals to the computers that control the flying surfaces (elevators, rudder etc.). The computer converts these to digital signals and processes them to determine what needs to move and by how much. The computer's decisions are then converted back to an analogue signal that operates the various **actuators**.

Sabbach, K. (1995), *21st Century Jet: The Making of the Boeing 777* (London: Pan Macmillan).

Anti-spam

Any software application, hardware or process that is used to combat the proliferation of **spam** or to keep spam from entering a system. Often provided as a free service by **ISP**s (Internet Service Providers) who wish to keep spam from blocking their systems.

See also **Bayesian filter**.

A

Anti-static device

Static electricity can affect computer systems. Static is easily built up, as car owners know, when the tyres rubbing on the road surface build up a static charge that gives the driver a shock when he or she leaves the car and provides a path between the metal body and the earth. Dissimilar fabrics used for clothes can produce such an effect, as can shoe soles on carpet. To avoid this happening and causing problems with a computer, anti-static wrist straps and floor mats can be employed. In its most extreme form static electricity manifests itself as lightning. In the case of lightning the charge that has been built up in the clouds discharges to earth. Lightning strikes can burn out delicate electrical components (**modems** are especially vulnerable), hence the need for anti-surge protection. Anti-static mats to prevent the build-up of static from shoes and carpets should form part of the consideration when designing **workstations**.

Anti-virus software

Specially designed software that detects and quarantines **viruses** and associated harmful programs such as **Trojans**. Given the increasing frequency of Internet-transmitted viruses, usually via email attachments, it is important that anti-virus software is updated on a regular basis. A number of commercial applications are available that automatically update a computer's protection each time it is logged onto the **Internet**. An annual fee for updating is often charged in addition to the purchase price. Some Internet Service Providers (**ISP**s) also provide a degree of virus protection by scanning **emails**.

See also **virus remedies** *and* **virus checkers**.

Applet

Applets are small, self-contained programs written in **Javascript**; they are executed by web **browsers** and allow the browser to execute the relevant **Java** program. The program may be a multimedia display, a game, a calculator, i.e. anything other than plain text or graphics, that requires the computer to carry out an executable command.

Applications/software

These are programs designed to carry out specific tasks (see the list below). They may be purchased as packages or specifically commissioned and written or adapted. For example, a major company may commission a database program to meet its own unique needs. Commercial packages may bundle together different types of applications so that the package contains, for instance, **word processing**, **spreadsheet** and **graphics** components.

A

Applications/software – audio

Programs that allow the user to manipulate audio material including speech and music. Material can be downloaded from the Internet and then uploaded onto personal music systems such as **MP3** players etc. Recent discussions between the music industry and those offering downloadable music have led to protocols whereby users pay a set amount for each track that is downloaded. This protects the artist who recorded the track as he or she will now receive royalties. It also protects the user from any charges that he or she has breached copyright.

Applications/software – CAD (Computer Aided Design)

Computer-aided design (CAD) uses computers to produce drawings in three dimensions and thus show the relationship in space between components. It also allows designers to make changes to designs easily and to see the implications of those changes.

In the mid-1990s the US aircraft manufacturer Boeing put together a massive amount of computer power in a system known as CATIA (Computer-graphics Aided Three-dimensional Interactive Application) and EPIC (Electronic Preassembly in the CATIA). EPIC allowed a computer model of the Boeing 777 airliner to be produced. CATIA was linked to component manufacturers across the globe so that the specifications of parts designed on the system were immediately available to them and could be fed, if necessary, directly to the machine tools (see **CAM (Computer Aided Manufacture)**).

Like most industrial operations, aircraft design is a process rather than an event and there are often many design changes. Before systems such as CATIA these might be posted, faxed or even hand-delivered. With the system used by Boeing, everybody concerned with that component would know of changes as soon as the new design was on the system. The time savings were immense.

As EPIC could spot any interference it meant that the finished product was much more likely to fit together properly, as it did. The whole process was documented in an excellent book, *21st Century Jet*, by Karl Sabbach and also in a joint US/UK television series. Sabbach reports how the computer checked for interferences on the 20 components that make up one of the 777's wing flaps. It made 207,601 checks and found 251 cases of interference. These might not have been discovered under the old system until an attempt was made to install the flap on the prototype, any problem then forcing the designers back to their drawing-boards.

Each component or major group of components was the responsibility of a DBT (Design Build Team) that could include remote members since the Internet and ICT facilitate the use of email and **videoconferencing** as easy and useful tools. No longer did designers have to take their drawings or models to a colleague on another floor or even another city or continent to see if it was OK. The whole process could now be carried out over a network of computers. Whilst this has not been an application much quoted, it must be one of the most important and ground-breaking uses of **networks** in recent time, holding forth as it does the prospect of global cooperation on design and manufacturing without any of the problems of distance, geography or time. No longer do designers have to waste precious hours on travelling.

The output from CAD programs is often to a special type of output device known as a **plotter**, which can produce very accurate drawings.

Sabbach, K. (1995), *21st Century Jet: The Making of the Boeing 777* (London: Pan Macmillan).

Applications/software – CAM (Computer Aided Manufacture)

The use of computers to direct and monitor manufacturing processes. Computers can control manufacturing tools and also monitor standards and specifications thus reducing the need for human interference. The instructions from the computer are relayed to **actuators** and motors that provide the necessary motion to machine tools. Computer Aided Manufacture can be linked to Computer Aided Design (**CAD**) directly so that the design system drives, at least in part, the machine tools making the component. CAM is of special use in situations where the materials used are hazardous as it lessens the exposure that humans may experience. CAM systems are replaceable even if expensive – humans are not!

See also **applications/software – (Computer Aided Design)**.

Applications/software – data analysis and statistics

Programs designed to perform statistical and data analysis operations such as calculating averages, standard deviation etc. Computers are able to produce results much faster than humans and are able to display results in a variety of graphical formats. The computer is also an ideal vehicle for 'what if?' scenarios as variables can be changed and the results examined very quickly and easily without losing the original data.

A

Applications/software – databases

Interrelated **data** stored together and accessible to a number of computer applications. A list of customers and their addresses is an example of a commonly used database. Databases are often included within other applications such as **word processing** software. The **mail merge** function in a word processor can access a database of addresses.

Databases are able to hold, collate and retrieve huge quantities of data and have greatly speeded up many routine data-handling tasks, thus freeing up people for more creative roles.

Applications/software – desk-top publishing (DTP)

DTP packages (for example Microsoft Publisher®) allow the user to set out text, graphics and photographs on screen in a professional manner akin to that of newspapers. Originally used by large commercial organizations, DTP applications are now cheap and easy enough for small business, voluntary organization and domestic use, especially given the relative ease of using colour.

Applications/software – games

For young and old alike there are a vast array of games ranging from adventure fantasies through to flight simulators and business games for use on either PCs or dedicated machines such as Playstation(™). Whilst many games are played for pure pleasure, the genre can overlap with simulations especially in respect of business games and simulations. As the means of presenting graphics has improved so has the sophistication of the games on offer for the computer user. The development and marketing of game software forms an important part of the ICT economy, employing a large number of programmers.

Applications/software – graphics

A

These programs manipulate drawings etc. usually for use within other applications or for printing out. **CAD** programs need a graphics component. Most **word processing** programs allow the user to import graphics or even to make simple drawings from the components of the word processing package.

Watson, J. (2000), *Drawing with Word* (London: Dorling Kindersley).

Applications/software – modelling

Computer packages that allow the user to model a situation and ask 'what if?' questions. Modelling is used to predict results especially where there may be dangers or problems in conducting live, real-time experiments. The behaviour of radioactive particles in a reactor can be modelled on a computer, as can the flow of crowds through a busy railway station. Modelling is highly dependent upon accurate data if it is to be effective. Modelling using computers has many of the same attributes as **simulations**.

Applications/software – photographs

It used to be a truism that the 'camera does not lie'. Nowadays, however, digitalization of photography allows the user to manipulate not only the quality but also the content of photographs. Expressions can be changed and items or people inserted or removed. **Digital** photographs can be emailed as attachments or sent via the latest generation of mobile **telephones**, provided that the telephone contains a camera. Programs such as Adobe Photoshop® are readily available and easy to use. Conventional photographs, including 35 mm slides, can be converted to digitalized form using a scanner. The scanner acts as an **analogue–digital converter** taking an **analogue** signal of colour, intensity and brightness and converting it to a set of **digital** pixels. The number of **pixels** that cameras generate has increased rapidly. Whilst 1 million was the norm just a short while ago, 6 million pixel cameras are rapidly becoming available at relatively affordable prices.

See also **digital cameras and camcorders**.

Towse, M. (2003), *The Complete Guide to Digital Photography* (London: Sanctuary).

Applications/software – presentation packages

Using computer programs such as PowerPoint® and a special projector, highly professional presentations mixing text, graphics, animation and photographs can be easily compiled on domestic or business computer equipment.

Whilst the ability to use mixed media is useful, it is important for presenters to remember that the message is the important thing and not the technology. Too many presentations are ruined by the overuse of functions. Dazzling the audience with technology can detract from the message. Despite the vast improvements in graphics quality, computer-generated photographs displayed on a large screen can appear flat and lifeless compared to 35 mm colour slides because the former uses **pixels** whilst the latter are composed of solid colour blocks. This problem will become less noticeable as the number of pixels to be displayed increases.

A

Applications/software – simulations

One of the best-known applications of a simulation is in aviation. Pilots transferring from one model of commercial jet airliner to another now undertake the vast majority of their training in a simulator. The computer operates not only the instruments but also **actuators** that move the whole simulator. By using this form of training risks are avoided and the trainers can manipulate a variety of situations and events. Simulation shares many facets with **modelling** in that it is used to replicate real life. Simulation, however, often replicates movements and is used for training in addition to 'what if?' situations.

Applications/software – spreadsheets

Spreadsheets are computer applications designed to manipulate and present mathematical operations. They are of especial use in accountancy packages (see Figure 3) and for **modelling** as they are ideal for 'what if?' situations, e.g. what will happen if annual growth is 3 per cent rather than 4 per cent. In this case it may only be necessary to alter one figure (that for percentage growth) and all other figures will be recalculated and displayed by the program.

Applications/software – stock control

Programs that are often linked to Electronic Point of Sale (**EPOS**) systems that allow users to keep careful track of stock and aid the reordering process. There is now no excuse for an organization to run out of stock. It has been calculated that the costs of storing and insuring stock can be up to 25 per cent of its value. Anything that saves the organization the need to store excess stock is to be welcomed. Just-in-Time systems operate by assessing needs and current holdings and ensuring that stock arrives just before it is needed thus saving on storage and insurance costs.

A

Applications/software – word processing

The manipulation of text using word processing software (e.g. Word®) is one of the most common uses of domestic and small business computers. Modern word processing programs are highly sophisticated and allow for the easy manipulation, display, formatting and printing of documents. Text may be written on a word processing program and then imported into other applications. In a similar manner graphics etc. can be imported into the word-processed documents. Word® is the most

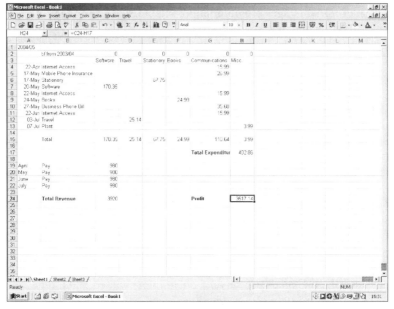

Figure 3   A spreadsheet

commonly used word processing program and its documents can be recognized by their .doc **file extension**.

Artificial intelligence (AI)

The ability of a computer to learn and improve performance through repeated experience. Artificial intelligence can be defined as the branch of computer science concerned with making computers behave like humans. The first use of the term 'artificial intelligence' was by John McCarthy at the Massachusetts Institute of Technology in 1956 although the ideas were first generated by the celebrated mathematician and code-breaker Alan Turing at Bletchley Park in the UK during the Second World War.

Artificial intelligence includes:

- games playing: programming computers to play games such as chess and other individual v. individual games requiring intellectual rather than physical prowess;
- expert systems: programming computers to make decisions in real-life situations (for example, expert systems can be used to assist doctors to diagnose diseases based on symptoms);

A

- natural language: programming computers to understand natural human languages;
- neural networks: systems that simulate intelligence by attempting to reproduce the types of physical connections that occur in animal brains;
- robotics: programming computers to see and hear and react to other sensory stimuli.

At the present time no computers can be said to exhibit full artificial intelligence (i.e., no matter how advanced the computer is it is unable to simulate the huge range of human behaviour). The greatest advances have occurred in the field of games playing. The best computer chess programs are now capable of beating humans. In May 1997, an IBM supercomputer called Deep Blue defeated world chess champion Gary Kasparov in a chess match. Interestingly the ancient Chinese game of Go has proved much more difficult for computers than chess.

In robotics computers are now widely used in assembly plants although the machines are capable only of very limited, often repetitive tasks. Robots have great difficulty identifying objects based on appearance or feel, and they still move and handle objects clumsily. In essence the ability of a computer to link sight and touch in the way a human brain does is severely limited. Mechanical advances have come nowhere near to matching the ability of the human (and all primates) to rotate the radius and the ulna (the two bones below the elbow) and to oppose the thumb and the forefinger. It is these primate abilities that give humans the incredible dexterity required for intricate tasks.

Natural-language processing offers the greatest potential rewards because it would allow people to interact with computers without needing any specialized knowledge. You could simply walk up to a computer and talk to it. Unfortunately, programming computers to understand natural languages has proved to be more difficult than originally thought. Some rudimentary translation systems that translate from one human language to another are in existence, but they are not nearly as good as human translators. There are also voice recognition systems, which can convert spoken sounds into written words. However, such systems only recognize word patterns and do not understand what has been said. In effect they are computerized dictation systems. Nevertheless, despite the limitations of such systems (the user needs to speak slowly and distinctly), the latest versions are capable of rudimentary learning in that they can recognize the user's particular diction (see **voice-activated software**).

In the early 1980s, expert systems were believed to represent the future of artificial intelligence and of computers in general and generated great excitement. To date, however, the promises have not been fulfilled. Many expert systems help human experts in such fields as medicine and engineering, but they are very expensive to produce and are helpful only in special situations.

Neural networks, which are proving successful in a number of disciplines such as voice recognition and natural-language processing are generating the most excitement in the early years of the twenty-first century.

There are several programming languages that are known as AI languages because they are used almost exclusively for AI applications. The two most common are LISP and Prolog.

ASCII (American Standard Code for Information Interchange)

A standard single-byte character encoding scheme used for text-based data. ASCII uses designated 7-bit or 8-bit number combinations to represent either 128 or 256 possible characters. Standard ASCII uses 7 bits to represent all uppercase and lowercase letters, the numbers 0 through 9, punctuation marks, and special control characters used in American English. Most current x86-based systems support the use of extended (or 'high') ASCII. Extended ASCII allows the eighth bit of each character to identify an additional 128 special symbol characters, foreign-language letters (including the £ sign for British English) and graphic symbols.

ASP (Active Server Page)

An ASP is a dynamically created web page with an .ASP extension that utilizes **ActiveX** scripting.

See also **URL**.

A

Assemblers

Assemblers are programs that translate assembly language components into **machine code** language that can be read by a computer. They are typically used by those writing programs and packages.

Asynchronous transmission

Asynchronous transmission refers to the transmission of characters along a channel at irregular intervals, an example being the input from a keyboard or from a microphone attached to **voice-activated software**.

ATM

See **Automatic teller machine (ATM)**

Attachments

Files, pictures etc. that are attached to an email and downloaded onto the **hard disk** or other storage device of the computer. Many **viruses** and other harmful programs are transmitted through seemingly harmless attachments.

Attributes

Characteristics assigned to all files and **directories**. Attributes include: Read Only, Archive, Hidden or System.

Audio

See **Applications/software – audio**

Automatic teller machine (ATM)

The term ATM originated in the USA although the machines are commonly referred to as 'cash points' or 'cash dispensers' in the UK. Operated by financial institutions (banks and building societies) ATMs are linked to the bank's central computers; they are operated using a bank card or credit card and allow cash withdrawals to take place and balances to be viewed. Originally only on bank sites, the machines are now to be found in retail outlets, hospitals and even on car ferries. Although the machines are highly efficient, recent concerns have centred on frauds that have taken place using card readers surreptitiously attached to the machine that can swipe the user's details coupled to a small camera also surreptitiously placed that can read the user's **PIN number**.

A

Back door

Back door is a feature that programmers often build into programs to allow special privileges normally denied to users of the program. Often programmers build back doors so they can fix **bugs**. If **hackers** or others learn about a back door, the feature may pose a security risk. Back door may also refer to a trap door. The back door idea has featured in a number of techno-thriller novels based on a programmer being able to gain access to a program he or she has written long after they have written it and maybe left the employ of the program owners. Unless well protected, back doors may provide hackers with a means of unauthorized access.

Background

This is the screen background image used on a Graphical User Interface (**GUI**) such as Windows®. Any pattern or picture that can be stored as a **bitmap** (.bmp) file can be set as a screen background.

Background task

A task executed by the system but generally remains invisible to the user. The system usually assigns background tasks a lower priority than foreground tasks. Some malicious software packages such as **viruses** and **trojans** are executed by a system as a background task so the user does not realize unwanted actions are occurring until it is too late as damage has already been caused.

Backup

A duplicate copy of data made for archiving purposes or for protecting against damage or loss. Backup also refers to the process of creating duplicate data (backing up). Some programs back up data files while maintaining both the current version and the preceding version on disk. However, a backup is not considered secure unless it is stored away from the original. Commercial organizations may arrange for storage of key data with companies whose sole task it is to provide high-security storage and backup facilities in case of major systems failure, accident or terrorist attack. Many organizations could go out of business if they lost records of their finances, customers and other vital information. Backup is not the same as saving. In the case of the latter the data still remains on the computer and thus is liable to damage. The idea of backing up is to have a separate, spare copy of data.

Bandwidth

In **analogue** communications bandwidth is the difference between the highest and lowest frequencies in a given range. For example, an analogue telephone line accommodates a bandwidth of 3000 hertz (Hz), the difference between the lowest (300 Hz) and highest (3300 Hz) frequencies it can carry. In **digital** communications, bandwidth is expressed in **bits** per second (bps).

Banner advertising

Advertisements that appear at the top of **search engines** etc. These advertisements are the means by which the developers of the search engines are able to make them available free of charge (see Figure 4 for an example). A number of changing advertisements may be used. Banner advertising may be annoying to some but it is what pays for the free search engines that have made net searching so easy for most users.

Bar codes

A series of machine-readable lines that are used to identify products by giving them unique **digital** codes. These codes can be read by a **bar code reader** and then used through **EPOS** (Electronic Point of Sale) to provide information for reordering and about customer buying patterns, in addition to registering the price at the till point.

Bar code readers

Optical devices that are able to read the **bar code** on a product and then feed the information to a central computer and till point. The information can then be used not only to display the price of the item but also to check remaining stocks and to reorder automatically if necessary. The bar code information can also be used in conjunction with the informa-

Banner

Figure 4   Banner advertisement on the Lycos homepage
Reproduced with permission of Lycos, Inc.

tion held on a **loyalty card** to build up a picture of the buying pattern of a particular user. This can then be used for targeted advertising.

Batch files

Text files containing one MS-DOS command on each line of the file. When run, each line executes in sequential order. The batch file AUTOEXEC.BAT is executed when the computer is booted and loads a series of controls and programs. This file type has the extension .bat.

Batch processing

Different from **real-time processing**, batch processing processes batches of information together and then either accepts or rejects the whole batch. Batch processing allows a large quantity of data to be dealt with at one time but imposes a delay as the system waits for the batches

B

to be assembled. In contrast, real-time processing occurs as the information comes in. Batch processing of (for example) invoices can be undertaken at night when the system is quieter.

Batch program

An **ASCII** (unformatted text) file that contains one or more operating system commands. A batch program's file name has a .cmd or .bat extension. When you type the file name at the command prompt, or when the batch program is run from another program, its commands are processed sequentially. Batch programs are also called batch files.

Baud rate

Named after the French engineer Jean-Maurice Emile Baudot and first used to measure the speed of telegraph transmissions. Today Baud is the number of frequencies or voltages made per second on a line. Baud should not be confused with bits or bytes. The baud rate indicates the speed at which a **modem** communicates. Baud rate refers to the number of times the condition of the line changes. This is equal to bits per second only if each signal corresponds to one bit of transmitted data.

Modems must operate at the same baud rate in order to communicate with each other. If the baud rate of one modem is set higher than that of the other, the faster modem usually alters its baud rate to match that of the slower one.

Bayesian filter

A means of identifying incoming email spam. Unlike other filtering techniques that look for spam-identifying words in subject lines and headers, a Bayesian filter considers the entire context of an **email** when it looks for words or character **strings** that will identify the email as spam. Another difference between a Bayesian filter and other content filters is that a Bayesian filter learns to identify new spam the more it analyses incoming emails. This 'learning' facility is used in the advanced spam prevention techniques used by Internet Service Providers to provide an automatic spam filtering service such as that provided by AOL (America On Line) 9.0 onwards. In this system the software recognizes some of the most common spam-type messages and also allows the user to list words that he or she finds in spam. Whenever a user reports a spam message the information is fed to the filter as part of its learning process.

B

Binary

Base 2 number system represented by the numeric values of 0 and/or 1. The importance of binary to Information and Communication Technology is that the two states can represent whether there is no current flowing (0) or a current flowing (1) in a **digital** system, the strength of the current (i.e. its **analogue** characteristics) being irrelevant. Using 1 and 0 all numbers can be represented in terms of a current on/off as shown below:

Base 10	Base 2 (binary)
0	0
1	1
2	10
3	11
4	100
5	101
6	110
7	111

BIOS (Basic Input–Output System)

The utility function held within a computer's read only memory (**ROM**) that contains the basic instructions for the operating system. BIOS is executed each time the computer is switched on.

Bitmap

Used for graphics including drawings and photographs, bitmaps comprise a fixed number of **pixels**, each of which is allocated a particular colour. Bitmap files can be saved using a variety of **file extensions** such as .bmp. Bitmap files take up much more space than, for example, a **JPEG** file. A file that requires 470 kB as a JPEG file needs 8184 kB in bitmap format.

Bits

The smallest element of data representation in a computer. The term is a contraction of **binary** data, i.e. either a 1 or a 0. A group of 8 bits makes up a byte.

An 8-bit hardware device or software program is one that is capable of transferring eight bits of data at the same time. When referring to a video card or graphics card 8-bit refers to the number of colours capable of being displayed. For example, 8-bit is the same as 256 colours (2 to the power of 8 = 256).

In a similar manner, a 16-bit hardware device or software program is one that is capable of transferring 16 bits of data at the same time. When referring to a video card or graphics card 16-bit refers to the number of colours capable of being displayed. For example 16-bit is the same as 65,536 colours (2 to the power of 16 = 65,536).

Similar calculations can be made for 24, 32 and 64 bits.

Blind copy

An **email** function that sends a copy of a message to another recipient without the original addressee knowing that a copy has been sent (cf. **carbon copy**).

Bluetooth

Bluetooth is a fairly recent idea that uses short-range radio waves to link peripherals to computers and headsets to mobile telephones. Bluetooth eliminates not only the need for wires but also the need for line-of-sight as required for the use of **infrared** beams. Bluetooth only works over relatively short distances.

Bookmarks

Also referred to as '**favourites**', bookmarks allow the user to record a **website** or page and then return to it with just one mouse click. This saves the user having to navigate his or her way back to a particular site or page and is thus useful for pages etc. that are visited on a frequent basis (see Figure 5). For example, the **homepage** for one's on-line banking is a prime candidate for bookmarking.

B

Boolean

Developed by the English mathematician and computer pioneer George Boole. Boolean algebra consists of operators such as 'AND', 'OR' or 'NOT'. Generally Boolean algebra is commonly used in programming and today in Internet **search engines**. For example, in a search engine someone may search for British AND Airways to look for British Airways.

Boolean expressions are expressions that result in the value of either TRUE/FALSE or YES/NO, 0/1 etc.

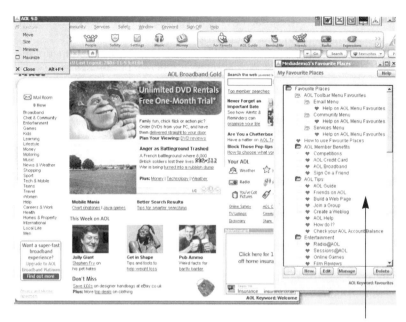

Favourites list

Figure 5   AOL homepage with the favourites list displayed
Reproduced with permission of AOL

Boot (system boot)

The process of loading the operating system from the **BIOS** when the computer is switched on each time. The term 'boot' is derived from 'bootstrap loader' (pulling oneself up by the bootstraps). Modern computers 'boot up' automatically as soon as they are switched on. In order for a computer to successfully boot, its **BIOS** operating system and hardware components must all be working properly as a failure of any one of these three elements is likely to result in a failed boot sequence.

When the computer's power is first turned on, the Central Processing Unit (**CPU**) initializes itself, which is triggered by a series of **clock ticks** generated by the system clock. Part of the CPU's initialization is to look to the system's **ROM** BIOS for its first instruction in the start-up program. The ROM BIOS stores the first instruction, which is the instruction to run the **Power On Self Test** (POST). POST then performs a check on the BIOS chip and then tests the **CMOS RAM**. If the POST does not detect a battery failure, it then continues to initialize the CPU, checking internal hardware devices such as the video card, secondary storage devices, such as **hard drives** and **diskette/zip drives**, ports and any

B

other hardware devices, such as the keyboard and **mouse/trackerball**, to ensure they are functioning properly.

Once the POST has determined that all components are functioning properly and the CPU has successfully initialized, the BIOS looks for an **operating system** (e.g. Windows® XP etc.) to load. The BIOS begins by looking to the CMOS chip to tell it where to find the operating system, and in most PCs the operating system is loaded from the C drive (i.e. the hard drive). However the BIOS possess the capability to load the operating system from a diskette, **CD** or a **zip** drive. The order of drives that the CMOS looks at in order to locate the operating system is known as the **boot sequence**, a sequence that can be changed by altering the CMOS setup. Looking at the appropriate boot drive, the BIOS will first encounter the **boot record**, which tells it where to find the beginning of the operating system and the subsequent program file that will initialize it.

Once the operating system initializes, the BIOS copies its files into memory and the operating system proceeds to take over control of the boot process. The operating system performs a further inventory of the system's memory and memory availability (which the BIOS already checked) and loads the device drivers that it needs to control the peripheral devices, such as a **printer**, **scanner**, optical (**CD/DVD**) drive, mouse and **keyboard**. The user can often tell that this process is underway as the various peripherals are initialized, a fact shown by the noise they make in doing so. This is the final stage in the boot process, after which the user can access the system's applications to perform tasks.

Booting the computer after it has been completely switched off is known as a cold boot.

Boot record/master boot record

The program recorded in the boot sector. This record contains information on the characteristics and contents of the disk and information needed to **boot** the computer. If a user boots a PC with a **diskette**, the system reads the boot record from that disk. The master boot record is the 340-**byte** program located in the **master boot sector**. This program reads the partition table, determines what partition to boot and transfers control to the program stored in the first sector of that partition. There is only one master boot record on each physical **hard disk**.

Boot sector/master boot sector

An area located on the first track of floppy disks and logical disks that contain the boot record. Boot sector usually refers to this specific sector of a diskette, whereas the term Master Boot Sector usually refers to the same section of a **hard disk**. This sector is located at sector 1, head 0, and track 0. The sector contains the **master boot record**.

Boot sequence

The order of **drives** that the **CMOS** looks to in order to locate the operating system.

Bridge

A bridge is used to connect two **Local Area Networks** (**LAN**) of the same type, as opposed to a **gateway** that links those of different types.

Broadband

Broadband refers to telecommunications that provide a variety of channels of data over a single wire. There are a wide variety of broadband technologies available in most areas, two of the more commonly found and used technologies are cable and ADSL broadband.

See also **ADSL**.

Browsers

Client programs that are used to navigate through the **World Wide Web**. Microsoft Explorer® is the most frequently used Internet browser. Browsers, often Microsoft Explorer®, are usually provided by **Internet Service Providers**. Browsers often allow the user to configure his or her own personal **homepage**.

To navigate through the web browsers use a series of navigational tools including BACK, FORWARD, HOME, **BOOKMARKS** and HISTORY (a list of viewed pages that remains until cleared by the user).

B

Bubble memory

This is a type of non-**volatile** memory composed of a thin layer of material that can be easily magnetized in only one direction. When a magnetic field is applied to a circular area of this substance that is not magnetized in the same direction, the area is reduced to a smaller circle, or bubble. For a period early in its development it was widely believed that bubble memory would become one of the leading memory technologies, but these promises have not been fulfilled. As it is, other non-volatile memory types, such as **EEPROM**, are faster and less expensive.

Buffer

Temporary memory in a computer or **printer** that collects bits of data until there is sufficient for processing. The text held on a clipboard is normally kept in a buffer. Unless instructed to the contrary buffers are cleared as soon as power is switched off. A buffer is a region of **RAM** reserved for use with **data** that is temporarily held while waiting to be transferred between two locations, such as between an application's data area and an input/output device.

Bugs

Bugs are programming faults that are usually discovered through use. The process of testing is known as **debugging**. As bugs become apparent, fixes or patches are made available (often on the Internet) in order to fix the problem. Although programmers take great care to avoid bugs, it is only in normal use that many problems become apparent.

Bundled software

Software that is included with a computer, hardware or related software. Generally this bonus software is at no additional cost. Much of **Microsoft's** early success was in getting its software accepted as bundles by the manufacturers of the computers the software was designed for and then providing not only the computer but also software bundled and pre-installed.

> *See also* **OEM (Original Equipment Manufacturer).**

B

Bus

In terms of Information and Communication Technology, the bus (also known as the address bus, data bus or local bus) is a data connection between two or more devices connected to the computer. For example, a bus enables a computer processor to communicate with the memory or a video card to communicate with the memory.

A bus is capable of being a **parallel** or a **serial** bus and today all computers utilize two types of buses, an internal or local bus and an external bus. An internal bus enables a communication between internal components such as a computer video card and memory and an external bus is capable of communicating with external components such as a **scanner**.

A computer or devices bus speed is measured in bits per second or megabytes per second.

Even the most basic home computer bought today will be equipped with a number of **USBs** (**Universal Serial Bus**) that allow easy connection of peripheral devices.

See also **networks**.

Bytes

A group of **bits** (usually eight) that are handled as a single unit of data by a computer. Memory is measured in bytes.

B

Cc

Cable modem

A device that enables a broadband connection to the **Internet** by using cable television infrastructure. Access speeds vary greatly, with a maximum throughput of 10 megabits per second (Mbps). The use of the cables originally installed for television is an excellent example of the **synergy** of ICT. By finding a new use for an existing facility it is possible to enhance the user's experience of his or her computer system at relatively little cost as well as removing the need for costly and time-consuming cable installations. If users could not access email and the Internet through existing telephone and television cables it is doubtful that ICT growth would have been as rapid as it has been.

Cache

An area in the computer's memory in which **web** pages are saved in order to speed up accessing them. As a cache fills up older files are removed to make way for newer ones.

CAD (Computer Aided Design)

See **applications/software – CAD (Computer Aided Design)**.

CAL (Computer Assisted Learning)

The use of a computer to train people in tasks using simulations, questioning etc.

CAM (Computer Aided Manufacture)

See **applications/software – CAM (Computer Aided Manufacture)**.

Carbon copy

A copy of an email sent to one or more third parties. Unlike a **blind copy** the original recipient is advised of who has received a copy.

Card reader

A card reader is attached to a computer and reads the memory card from a **digital camera or camcorder**, transferring the data to the computer where it can be manipulated and stored for subsequent retrieval or sending via email.

CBT (Computer Based Training)

Similar to **CAL** but with a wider, more developmental focus.

CD/CD(R)/CD(RW) – Compact disks

Standard CDs are usually 'read only'. A CD(R) disk can be written to but files may not be removed, provided that the computer has a suitable drive. CD(RW) disks can be used as floppy disks. The advantages of CDs is that they can store much more information than floppy disks and yet are relatively light in weight. They are also less susceptible to corruption as they are written to optically not magnetically. This also gives much more storage space than a magnetic **diskette** (other than an **Iomega Zip** or **Iomega Jaz** disk) and they are able to be accessed much more quickly.

CD-ROM

Compact disks with a read only memory that cannot be written to. Most software applications come on a CD-ROM, ensuring that the user cannot inadvertently erase any of the data.

Censorship

Censorship refers to restrictions placed on who can see what. The Internet has made censorship very difficult. Certain material may be illegal in particular jurisdictions. Most **Internet Service Providers** provide parental controls that act as **child protection facilities** so that parents can restrict the type of material that their children can view.

Totalitarian governments that have traditionally practised strict censorship have found the growth of the **Internet** problematic as their control over content and access has been very much restricted, given the growth of automatic telephone services that mean anybody with a computer and a **modem** can have access to the Internet and the uncensored material that it contains.

C

Certificate

A **digital** document that is commonly used for authentication and secure exchange of information on open networks, such as the Internet, **extranets** and intranets. A certificate securely binds a public key to the entity that holds the corresponding private key. Certificates are digitally signed by the issuing certification authority and can be issued for a user, a computer or a service. The most widely accepted format for certificates is defined by the ITU-T X.509 version 3 international standard. The binding of the public and private keys is an important part of the security process especially where financial information is being sent via email and the Internet. They also ensure that only those who are authorized to obtain information can do so.

CGI

CGI is short for both:

Common Gateway Interface, allowing users visiting a web page to send and receive information from a server. For example, CGI script can be used to allow a user to type a set of **keywords**, pass those keywords to a CGI application to process a search, and then return results based off the search to the web page.

and:

Computer Generated Image (sometimes abbreviated to CG) – any image or sequence of images that have been generated with the aid of computers.

Charge Coupled device (CCD)

A type of electronic light sensor used within **digital cameras** to capture a scene and turn it into a **digital** picture.

Chat rooms

Chat rooms are a development of the Internet that allow a group of people to post messages and chat in real time. They are virtual rooms set in cyberspace. Chat rooms may be public or private. A public chat room often brings together people with a common interest to share thoughts, or allows a celebrity to answer questions. Even governments have been known to use chat rooms to elicit views. Chat rooms need to be mediated in order to ensure that standards of behaviour are adhered to. Private chat rooms involve just a few individuals chatting between themselves and are **password** protected. **Internet Service Providers** (**ISPs**) such as America On Line (AOL) also offer chat facilities via public forums or the ability to set up private chats with other members (known as 'buddy chat' on AOL). The use of chat rooms by young people has become a matter of concern as it is difficult to ascertain the age of those using the facilities and there have been cases of older predators 'grooming' young people in chat rooms and suggesting that they arrange meetings.

Child protection facilities

There is a growing need for parents to control the use of the Internet by children. Most **Internet Service Providers** (**ISPs**) provide password-protected settings that allow parents to restrict the sites that their children can access (see Figure 6).

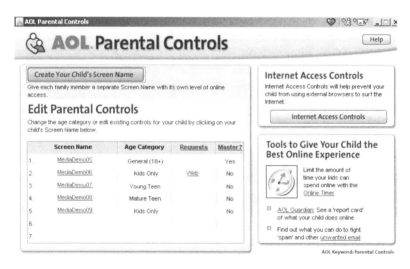

Figure 6   The parental controls on AOL (America On Line)
Reproduced with permission of AOL

Chip and PIN

Credit and debit card fraud (£400 million per year in the UK alone) has increased significantly in most countries over the past few years. This is mainly due to the huge increase in the number of cards now in circulation, as well as the fact that plastic cards are being used more and are now accepted in so many places. The card-issuing institutions have developed chip and PIN as a step forward from the acceptance of just a signature as proof of identity. Whilst a signature should be unique it is very easy for the salesperson in a busy shop to give the signed payment slip only a cursory glance.

Chip and **PIN** is an industry-wide initiative backed by the UK and other governments in order to protect cardholders from card crime. Chip and PIN cards contain embedded computer chips (an extra impact on fraudsters is that the chip makes a card much harder and more expensive to counterfeit). The UK has been rather slow in adopting chip and PIN; it has already been in use in some countries for up to 10 years and has been proven to cut card fraud by as much as 80 per cent.

Chip and PIN means simply entering a **PIN number** into a hand-sized keypad when the card is used for face-to-face transactions (e.g. in shops, restaurants, supermarkets, petrol stations, etc.):

- The card will be inserted into a card reader or PIN pad.
- After checking the amount, the cardholder enters his or her PIN discreetly (the PIN pads have a shield to stop others seeing the number).
- The machine will then check the PIN entered against the PIN held on the chip in your card, just as the signature on a receipt is checked against the signature on the card today.
- The user will be given a receipt for his or her purchases.

From 1 January 2005, if a chip and PIN-enabled card is used fraudulently at a retailer facility that has not been chip and PIN-enabled, the retailer will be liable for the loss. Thus there has been a considerable incentive for retailers to ensure that they had chip and PIN technology in place by 2005.

PIN pads comply with the standards set by the Royal National Institute for the Blind and have a raised dot on the number 5 key (as do telephones). Retailers are obliged to put PIN pads where customers are able to reach them

It may be easier for some customers to enter their PIN than to sign as they do now, which will aid those with disabilities.

See also **PIN numbers** *and* **Disability and ICT**.

Client

In terms of **ICT** a client is any computer or program connecting to, or requesting the services of, another computer or program. Client can also refer to the software that enables the computer or program to establish the connection. For a **local area network** (**LAN**) or the **Internet** a client is a computer that uses shared network resources provided by another computer known as a **server**.

Clip art

Commercially available art for use with computers. Clip art usually consists of multiple images which the user can import into his or her own work. Some clip art images may be pre-loaded onto a system whilst others are accessed from purchased disks.

Clipboard

The location in a computer operating system such as Microsoft Windows® that stores information that has been cut or copied from a document or other location. The clipboard will hold this information until it has been overwritten by new information. For example, a user may copy information from a **word processor** and paste that information into an email. Many operating systems include software utilities known as a clipboard viewer that enable a user to see what information is currently being stored in the clipboard, set up the clipboard with permissions and/or view the history of the clipboard. If there is a large amount information on the clipboard before the computer is switched off the user is asked whether he or she wishes this information to be available to other applications later.

Clock speed

Clock speed refers to the number of cycles per second that the **processor** of a computer operates at. More than anything, it is increases in clock speed that have led to the most dramatic increases in processing power. Initially measured in megahertz (millions of cycles per second), modern processors have reached gigahertz capabilities. An 800 MHz processor operates with a clock running at 800 million cycles per second. Modern processors can often complete multiple instructions during each **cycle**. The faster the processor runs, the more it can accomplish in a given time.

C

Clock tick

A clock tick is also known as a **cycle** and is the smallest unit of time recognized by a device. For personal computers, clock ticks generally refer to the main system clock, which runs at 66 MHz. This means that there are 66 million clock ticks (or cycles) per second. Since modern **CPU**s run much faster (up to 3 GHz), the CPU can execute several instructions in a single clock tick.

CMOS (Complementary Metal Oxide Semiconductor)

Pronounced 'see-moss', CMOS is a widely used type of semiconductor. CMOS semiconductors use both NMOS (negative polarity) and PMOS (positive polarity) circuits. Since only one of the circuit types is on at any given time, CMOS chips require less power than chips using just one type of **transistor**. This makes them especially attractive for use in battery-powered devices, such as portable computers. Personal computers also contain a small amount of battery-powered CMOS memory to hold the date, time and system setup date. CMOS devices are also used to capture digital photographs (see **digital cameras**).

COBOL (Common Business Oriented Language)

A high-level programming language used for business and file-handling programs.

Codec

Codec stands for compression/decompression. A codec is an **algorithm** or special computer program that reduces the number of bytes consumed by large files such as those used for audio and video (see **MPEG**). Codecs are often used with videos distributed over the Internet and enable what would normally be a very large video file to be much smaller for downloading. Codecs themselves can be downloaded from the Internet (see Figure 7).

In communication a codec is short for coder/decoder, that is, a chip that decodes analogue-to-digital conversion and digital-to-analogue.

Command lines

Each instruction to a computer for a task is composed of lines of commands. Each line provides a specific instruction for the program to do or check for something.

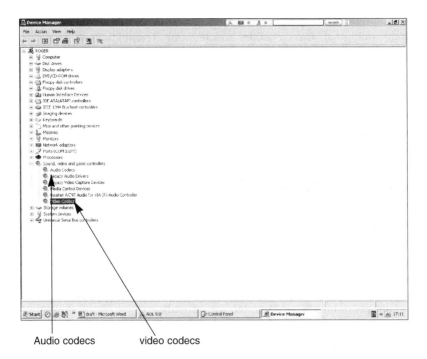

Audio codecs   video codecs

Figure 7   Codecs listed through Windows® device manager (reached through; Control panel – System – Hardware – Device Manager)

Communication

Communication is the process of receiving and transmitting data and information. From simple face-to-face speech through written messages to **networked** computers and the Internet, the communication's process follows a similar format, as shown in Figure 8.

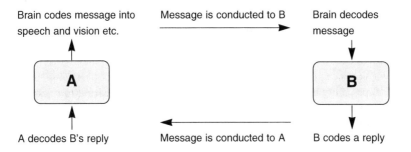

Brain codes message into speech and vision etc.

Message is conducted to B

Brain decodes message

A

B

A decodes B's reply

Message is conducted to A

B codes a reply

Figure 8   Communications model

A and B may be people or computers (although at the input and ultimate output of any computer is a person). The input may be via a keyboard, voice input, scanner etc. This then needs to be coded into a digital message that can be processed and transmitted by the computer. Anything that interferes with the transmission process is known as **noise**. Noise does not have to be an auditory phenomenon. A visual occurrence that distracts the attention of a person engaged in a conversation can be classed as noise, as can any degradation of the telephone line linking a computer via a **modem** to a **network**.

Communication port

A port on a computer that allows asynchronous communication of one byte at a time. A communication port is also known as a serial port.

Communications server

A network server dedicated to the communications process that manages communications across the network.

Compatibility

Compatibility refers to the ability of programs and peripherals to work with newer or older versions, i.e. they are compatible with each other. There are two types of compatibility:

- backwards compatibility;
- forwards compatibility.

Backwards compatibility means that something will work with an older version. For example Word® 6 could read an earlier Word® format file. An Iomega 250 MB zip drive can read both 250 MB zip disks and the older 100 MB version. Forwards compatibility commonly means that an older version can use something newer. Internet Cleanup works with newer versions of AOL as well as the version running when it was installed. Older versions of Word® could not always read files written in newer versions, i.e. they were not always forward compatible.

Compatibility is very important when upgrading software and operating systems. There would be little point in upgrading to Windows® XP if one could not open files written when the operating system being used was Windows® ME.

Compilers

Programs that translate high-level source codes (COBOL, Pascal etc.) into machine code for use in the **CPU**. Unlike **interpreters**, compilers do not directly execute program statements.

Compression

A compressed file is one that has been 'squeezed' to take up less memory. It cannot be accessed in this form but can be transmitted electronically and then uncompressed for use.

See also **zip**.

Computer types – desktop

The desktop computer usually consisting of a **CPU** (central processing unit), keyboard, monitor, printer, scanner etc. is the type of computer most widely used for domestic and business purposes. Over time the machines have become faster and contain more memory whilst the price has dropped in relative terms. Today's desktop machines have **CD/DVD** drives in addition to floppy disk drives.

Computer types – embedded

More and more seemingly simple domestic appliances such as washing machines contain embedded microchips that control and monitor functions. A modern motor vehicle may contain a number of embedded computer chips. One of the fears of the year 2000 was that such chips might fail when the date changed from 1999 to 2000 although this did not happen in reality. Embedded microchips perform their function without any action from the user save for the normal selection of functions – in effect the user is unaware of their presence unless, of course, the chip malfunctions. Even then replacement may be a very simple operation.

C

Computer types – laptop

A portable form of the desktop computer, laptops are slightly more expensive but contain the same features. Being portable they need greater protection from accident and a flat screen rather than the traditional cathode ray monitor.

Computer types – mainframe

Mainframe computers are large computers, typically costing millions of pounds, that are capable of large-scale simultaneous processing. They are used for large-scale data processing and scientific applications as well as acting as **network servers** for desktop computers.

Computer types – notebook

A smaller type of laptop that tends to cost more due to increased miniaturization. Notebook computers may have fewer drives etc. than the corresponding laptop.

Computer types – PDA (Personal Digital Assistants)

These are very small, hand-held computers that at their simplest are just electronic diaries, calculators and address books. The more complex versions may have facilities for **synchronizing** with a desktop/laptop and a keyboard facility. One of the disadvantages of the PDA is the need to use a stylus on a **touchscreen** for input (unless a keyboard – taking up space – is attached). The small size of the screen may also present problems for some users.

Computer types – supercomputers

Supercomputers are used for tasks that require huge amounts of computing power. Like all computers they have become smaller and more powerful but in the case of supercomputers smallness means that they only take up a room rather than a whole building! Governments make considerable use of supercomputers, especially for defence simulations. Amongst the best known are the Cray supercomputers used by a number of US government agencies.

Conditional Control Transfer Capability

A computer capability that allows commands to be executed in any order, not just the order in which they were programmed.

Config.sys

Config.sys is a file used with MS-DOS and OS/2 and is **booted** up when the computer is first booted up; it controls components hooked up to the computer such as memory and other hardware devices.

Connection speed

The speed with which the computer is connected to the telephone network via a modem. A typical dial-up (as opposed to **Broadband**) connection is of the order of 56,000 (56 K) bytes per second.

Consumables

Those items such as paper, labels, toner, inkjet cartridges and even floppy disks that are consumed during computing operations.

Control Panel

Control Panel is a Windows® function of specialized tools that are used to change the way Windows® looks and behaves (see Figure 9). Some of these tools are for adjusting settings that personalize the computer use, such as changing the standard mouse pointers with animated icons that move on the screen, or using Sounds and Audio Devices to replace standard system sounds with sounds chosen by the user. Other tools help set up Windows® so the computer is easier to use. For example, left-handed users can switch the mouse buttons so that the button on the right performs the primary functions of selecting and dragging.

Figure 9   Windows® XP Control Panel

Cookies

Cookies are blocks of text placed in a file on your computer's hard disk. Websites use cookies to identify users who revisit the site.

Cookies might contain log-in or registration information, shopping basket information from e-commerce or user preferences. When a server receives a browser request that includes a cookie, the server can use the information stored in the cookie to customize the website for the user so as, for example, to provide a personalized welcome. Cookies can be used to gather more information about a user than would be possible without them. Cookies take up very little memory.

Copyright

Copyright assigns ownership of material to individuals and companies. Most countries have strict copyright laws. The use of copyrighted material for commercial gain or even for non-profit making purposes is usually prohibited. Unless it is stated that it is **shareware**, the content of most websites and all software is copyright protected, i.e. copies cannot be made. Many software programs will allow one copy to be made for backup purposes. If the user wishes to place a program on a second computer, a new copy should be purchased. The ability to download music has led to threats of legal action as this can deprive the performers of their royalties.

CPU (Central Processing Unit)

The control and arithmetic/logic unit of a computer. Basically the CPU is the place where data is sent for processing and where information is released to the peripherals after processing.

Customizing

The process of adapting commands (through Control Panel for users of Windows®) to suit the individual user. Within programs it is possible to customize. Word® allows the user to set up spelling/grammar preferences and to compile a customized dictionary in addition to choosing favourite fonts etc. for new documents.

Cybercafé

Commercial premises that provide Internet access for the public. Many of these establishments also provide refreshments, as the name implies.

The smallest may have just a few terminals whilst large operators such as easyCafe provide banks and banks of terminals at a very low cost. Cybercafés can be found in almost every town and city in the world including the foot of Mount Everest and on cruise ships and other modes of transport. Whilst they do not always offer refreshment, the term 'cybercafé' has become generic although 'cyber study' is also used for those facilities on ships and in hotels where access is granted only to passengers and residents.

Cycle

See **clock tick**.

C

Data

Data is basic facts that need to be interpreted to become **information** and thus meaningful (see Figure 10).

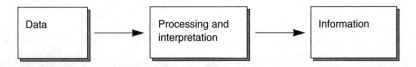

Figure 10   Data in – information out

Data analysis and statistics

See **applications/software – data analysis and statistics.**

Data identification

The key task of deciding which data is relevant. The old adage of GIBO (garbage in – garbage out) applies (or RIBO, rubbish in – rubbish out). One can only obtain information out that is as good as the data that went in.

Data link

See **data transmission.**

Data processing

The process of manipulating data so that the result is meaningful information. Computers are highly efficient at looking for patterns etc. from a stream of data and putting the resulting information into a form that can be used.

Data switch

A switch used to determine where data goes. A computer that has, for example, a laser printer and an inkjet printer (see under **printer** for both) attached can use a data switch between the computer port and the printers, thus allowing them both to use the same port depending on the task in hand – the laser printer for normal documents, the inkjet printer when colour is required. In the example cited it may be necessary to 'tell' the program being used which printer is intended to receive the data so that the correct drivers will be used.

Data transmission

The electronic transfer of data along telephone lines, **fibre optic cables** or by the use of **infra red** or radio waves.

Such links can allow one computer to operate systems in conjunction with another in order to maximize effectiveness. An early example of this was demonstrated in 1982 during the conflict between the UK and Argentina. In order to protect the British task force anchored in San Carlos Bay after the landing of 3 Commando Brigade, the Royal Navy stationed two ships out to sea to pick up enemy aircraft on radar and then to engage them with surface-to-air (SAM) missiles. Unfortunately the ships equipped with suitable missiles (Type 42 destroyers) had inadequate range and the ships with the most up-to-date radar fit (Type 22 frigates) had only short-range missiles. The solution was to datalink the radar data from the Type 22 to the missile control systems of the Type 42 using a wireless data link (see Figure 11 on p. 44). Unfortunately the Argentinian forces soon realized the potency of linking in this way and HMS *Coventry* was sunk during a carefully planned air attack that overwhelmed the defences.

Hastings, M. and Jenkins, S. (1983), *The Battle for the Falklands* (London: Michael Joseph).

D

Database Management System (DBMS)

The software program used to control the use of a **database**.

Databases

See applications/software – databases.

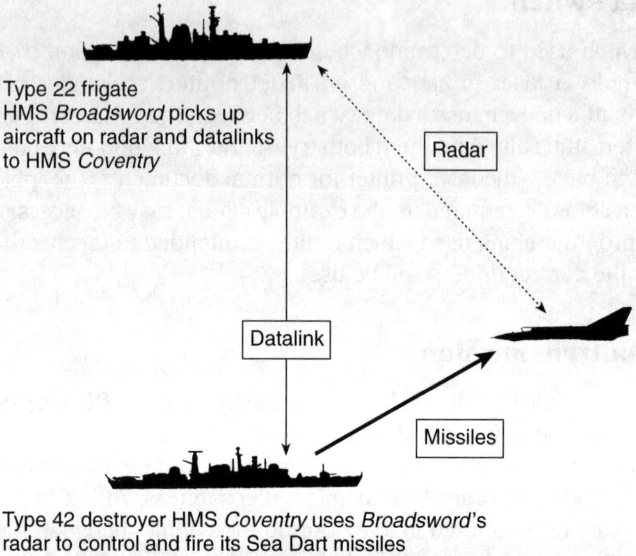

Type 22 frigate
HMS *Broadsword* picks up
aircraft on radar and datalinks
to HMS *Coventry*

Radar

Datalink

Missiles

Type 42 destroyer HMS *Coventry* uses *Broadsword*'s
radar to control and fire its Sea Dart missiles

Figure 11 Datalink in use in the Falklands conflict in 1982

Dates

Dates have the appearance of **strings** and there are times when the computer treats them as such. At other times, however, dates need to be processed as **real numbers**. This occurs when days are added to a date etc. Dates, however, are not base 10 numbers as some months have 28/29, 30 or 31 days. The computer is able to handle this through its programming. As the year 2000 approached there was global concern that many of the world's computers and devices using microchips, such as domestic appliances, might crash. The reason for the concern was that many programs (especially early ones) had been written with only the last two digits of the year used to save memory. Hence 20 March 1995 was programmed in as 20.03.95 and not 1995. The concern was that on 01.01.2000 the computer would believe that time had gone backwards and that 01.01.00 was in reality 1900. Companies and governments appointed Y2K (Year 2000) compliance officers to check systems. In the event there appeared to be no problem at all – the vast majority of computers carried on working with the dates correctly adjusted.

Debugging

The process of testing a program under working conditions to remove problems and **bugs**. Much debugging occurs before a new piece of software or an upgrade is launched but there are nearly always bugs remaining that only manifest themselves in normal use. As soon as the developers hear of these bugs they can debug them and provide downloadable **patches** to rectify the problem.

Decision Support Systems (DSS)

The use of spreadsheets, statistical packages etc. that allows individual mangers to access the information they need for decisions without the need to refer to central **management information systems**. The use of more stand-alone packages allows greater flexibility but may suffer from the lack of wider access to other material.

Default user

The profile that serves as a basis for all user profiles. Every user profile begins as a copy of the default user profile, which can then be changed to a specific user profile.

Defragmentation

Defragmentation is the process of rewriting parts of a file to contiguous sectors on a hard disk to increase the speed of access and retrieval (see drives – hard). When files are updated, the computer tends to save these updates on the largest continuous space on the hard disk, which is often on a different sector from the other parts of the file. When files are thus fragmented, the computer must search the hard disk each time the file is opened to find all of the file's parts, which slows down response time.

Desk-top publishing (DTP)

See applications/software – desk-top publishing.

D

Device drivers

Usually referred to as a driver, a device driver is a group of files that enable a hardware device such as a **printer**, external drive (**Zip**, **Jaz**, **CD**, **DVD** etc.), **scanner** etc. to communicate with the computer's operating system. Drivers are usually included as a software package with a new device or can be downloaded from the manufacturer's **website**. Drivers for commonly used equipment such as printers that are easily obtained in the marketplace may be included as part of the software package supplied with the computer. Most computers contain the necessary drivers for Canon, HP, Lexmark and other printers.

Dial up

The process of activating a modem and dialling out to a server in order to connect up to the Internet.

Dial-up connection

When connecting via the **telephone network** the dial-up connection includes **modems** with a standard phone line, **ISDN** cards with high-speed ISDN lines, or **ADSL/broadband** modems. With the latter the connection can be permanent and still allow the telephone to be used.

Digital

Any system that uses a series of discrete numbers for display or processing rather than a variable **analogue** form. Digital systems may use a binary system with just two digits, 1 and 0 or a hexadecimal system based on 16 discrete values, 0 to 9 and A to F.

A two-position light switch is a good example of a **binary** digital device. When the switch is off, no electricity reaches the light. When it is on all of the available current is used for the light which is illuminated to its maximum. It can be replaced by an analogue dimmer switch whereby the amount of illumination can be varied infinitely by rotation of the switch, i.e. by altering the current passed to the light. Figure 12 shows a digital system relating to sound.

The effects of a digital signal can be seen easily in digital television. The traditional analogue signal could lead to ghosting and deterioration

D

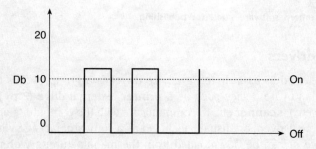

Figure 12   A digital system that switches on a device when sound exceeds 10 decibels

in quality if the signal strength diminished. Digital suffers from no such problem. The high-quality picture is dependent purely on whether there is a signal being received or not; the strength of the signal is of no importance. If, however, the signal is not received there is no picture and sound at all. With an analogue signal quality diminishes as a function of signal strength; with digital there is either perfect quality or nothing.

Digital cameras and camcorders

Digital cameras and camcorders use computer technology to generate a picture using **pixels**. In part a digital camera works by opening a shutter to allow light to enter the camera. The difference is that rather than the light falling on a film, it falls on a light-sensitive **CCD** or **CMOS**. The tiny sensors on their surface convert the image electronically into picture elements – pixels – which, when combined, make up the complete image.

The number of effective pixels offered by digital cameras has risen dramatically. Where 1 million pixels was the norm not many years ago, 6 million pixel-plus cameras are now readily available. The more pixels, the better the resolution and thus the higher the quality of the image.

More advanced digital photography uses a mixture of optical and digital techniques. An example is in the use of zoom function. Optical zoom needs more light but the resolution remains the same. Digital zoom loses **resolution**. A camera with 12 times zoom may achieve this through 3 times optical zoom and 4 times ($3 \times 4 = 12$) digital zoom. The top-of-the-range digital cameras use optical single lens reflex technology linked to a digital function to replace the film.

Digital photographs and video are stored on the camera's memory card and the images required are **downloaded** onto a computer (many cameras allow basic editing) and then they can be edited, sent via email or printed.

Many photographers still prefer to use traditional film, especially 35mm slide film. Slide film contains complete blocks of colour rather than pixels and thus has a very high resolution. This is seen to good effect when comparing a slide beamed onto a screen and a digital image, say through PowerPoint®. The latter often appears flatter and less well defined compared to the older slide technology. The advantage of using presentation programmes, of which PowerPoint® is probably the most widely employed, is that text can be added, as can animation. Editing is easy and a number of presentations can be held on a single **compact disk** (**CD**) avoiding the need to carry 35mm slides around. On its own a single slide does not weigh much but 400–500 can make a considerable dent in the carry-on baggage allowance granted by airlines.

D

Digital signature

A digital signature is a means for originators of a message, file or other **digitally** encoded information to bind their identity to the information. The process of digitally signing information entails transforming the information, as well as some secret information held by the sender, into a tag called a signature. Digital signatures are used in public key environments, and they provide non-repudiation and integrity services.

Direct Memory Access (DMA)

The transfer of **data** in blocks instead of character by character without the need for continuous control by the processor. DMA is possible whenever peripheral devices such as external **drives** are able to operate autonomously using DMA software. All the processor needs to specify is the start address of the data to be transferred and its length. The processor is then available for other tasks although it will run at a slightly slower speed.

Directories

Directories are the addresses on the **hard disk** where related **files** are stored. A directory is not a specific defined physical area on the hard disk. Files that have a particular directory address may be stored on various sectors on the disk; they need not be located in a contiguous manner. For example, the directory C:/windows/office/word/books may contain files named:

    C:/windows/office/word/books/ICT/definitions
    C:/windows/office/word/books /ICT/draft
    C:/windows/office/word/books/ICT/synopsis

Where files are physically located is unimportant. The computer can access the files via their addresses and knows that they are all linked to the same directory. It is the high speed of accessing material on a hard disk that allows files to be spread over the disk without inconveniencing the user.

For directories on the Internet see **web directories**.

Disability and ICT

The renowned Nobel Prize-winning (and disabled) physicist Steven Hawking has demonstrated how effective use of Information and Communication Technology can help those suffering from disabilities to contribute and gain as much from life and society as everybody else. ICT can remove the need to travel to and from a workplace. Users can communicate using **touchscreens, voice-recognition software** and even (in the case of Hawking) voice synthesizers.

Braille **keyboards** linked to audio facilities and increased font size can aid those with sight problems and even those unable to operate a keyboard can control a computer and communicate using **voice-recognition software**. **Touchscreens** can remove the need to use a keyboard.

The use of microprocessors to aid those with mobility problems through the use of **actuators** linked to nerve functions is an exciting area of study, linking as it does ICT, biology and medicine. A further application of ICT in this area is in the monitoring of those with disabilities, enabling them to live more normal lives in the community.

PIN pads and telephones should comply with the standards set by the Royal National Institute for the Blind (RNIB) and have a raised dot on the number 5.

Cartwright, R (2002), *Express-Exec Empowerment* (Oxford: Capstone).

Disaster recovery management

Procedures that companies and individuals put into place to recover **data** lost through accident or malicious attack. At its simplest this may take the form of **backup** copies of **files** held on **external drives** and **disks**. At its most sophisticated it may involve the sending of **data** to remote locations and secure storage facilities off site in specially constructed facilities. Such facilities may be bomb- and EMP (**electromagnetic pulse**)-proof. As more and more use is made of computers so the need to ensure security of data held electronically increases. Whilst secure storage might be expensive the loss of data to a large organization may be catastrophic.

Specialist organizations exist that can recover data from damaged hard disks or data that has been accidentally deleted (completely erasing data is not all that easy as a trace remains on the hard disk until written over by new data). It is surprising how much can be recovered from a disk that is seemingly damaged beyond repair.

D

Disinfection

A process used by most **anti-virus software** after reporting the presence of a **virus** to the user. During disinfection, the virus may be removed from the system and, whenever possible, any affected data recovered.

Disk

A modern PC contains a hard disk at the core of the **CPU**. The hard disk contains the Read Only Memory (**ROM**) and is also used for storing files. Disk storage capacity now routinely exceeds 40 GB, a considerable advance on the smaller-capacity disks of the 1990s. Prior to the introduction of hard disks, PCs had to have the operating system loaded from one of the original 5-inch floppy disks each time the computer was switched on, the CPU only containing the instructions for loading the operating system in its memory. The hard disk is divided into sectors.

See also **hard disk drive** *and* **diskette**.

Diskette (also known as a floppy disk)

A 3.5 inch diskette drive for reading and writing to and from the computer is now a standard feature of PCs. In the 1980s many machines had to use audio tape cassettes to save and retrieve data – a time-consuming process and one prone to corruption. The next stage was the 5.25 inch floppy disk, a device that greatly speeded up the loading and saving of data and programs. Within a few years the enclosed 3.5 inch diskette with its protective plastic case had been developed. Easily sent through the post or kept in a pocket, the diskette has been superseded for many uses by **zip** drive disks and compact disks. The zip drive disk operates in a similar manner to a diskette. By using magnetic readers and media, it is relatively easy to read, write and rewrite to the diskette. Diskettes have a storage capacity of 1.44 MB; this makes them somewhat inadequate for use with media files that often exceed this size. Compression, using programs such as Winzip, of files can increase the storage capacity of diskettes by a factor of up to 3.5.

Distributed processing

Distributed processing relies on a network of geographically separate computers rather than a centralized central computer. Distributed processing allows an organization to use spare capacity within its network for tasks that would otherwise involve the expense of a centralized computer. In the event of a malfunction, other computers within the network can take on the tasks of the malfunctioning unit.

DOS and MS-DOS (Disc Operating Systems)

DOS is short for Disk Operating System and is the common term used to describe MS-DOS, Microsoft's disk operating system.

The initial versions of DOS were very simple and resembled another operating system known as CP/M (Control Program for Microcomputers; created by Digital Research Corporation, CP/M was one of the first 8-bit operating systems for personal computers). Subsequent versions have become increasingly sophisticated. DOS is still a 16-bit operating system and does not support multiple users or multi-tasking.

For some time now, it has been widely acknowledged that DOS is insufficient for modern computer applications. Microsoft Windows® up to Windows® 95 helped alleviate some problems, but it still sat on top of DOS and relied on DOS for many services. Even Windows® 95 sat on top of DOS. Newer operating systems do not rely on DOS to the same extent, although they can execute DOS-based programs. It is expected that as these operating systems gain market share, DOS will eventually disappear.

Docking devices

A base unit attached to the computer (usually through a **USB** port) that allows cameras etc. to be connected to the computer in order to download data. Stand-alone digital photography printers are now on the market that do not need a computer but which interface directly with the camera and print off photographs.

Domain names

A domain name identifies and locates a host computer or services on the Internet.

The Domain Name Service (DNS) allows Internet hosts to be organized around domain names: for example, amazon.com is a domain assigned to the Internet book, music and electronic seller Amazon with the suffix 'com' signifying a commercial organization. Logging on to www.amazon.com will take you to the main Amazon site in the USA. There are also a number of other Amazon sites located in different countries, as illustrated by the activity below. As it is possible to search for a book on the Amazon site without needing a password (one will be needed if a purchase is to be made), the Amazon operation is a useful example for this lesson.

The suffix .com is called a generic top-level domain name, and up to 2001 there were only:

D

.com   company/commercial organization

.net   Internet gateway or administrative host
.mil   military
.org   non-profit making organization
.edu   educational institutions
.gov   government agencies
.ac   further and higher educational institutions in the UK
.co   some commercial organizations in the UK or New Zealand

As a result of the rapid growth in **Internet** use, seven new names –
.biz, .aero, .coop, .info, .pro, .museum and .name – are now being used.
In order to increase the number of domains available, there is also a
discrete code for each country although this is not always used, especially where the .com and the later domains are concerned. Examples of
the country codes are:

.au   Australia
.ca   Canada
.de   Germany
.fr   France
.jp   Japan
.nl   Netherlands
.ru   Russia
.uk   United Kingdom

Domain Name System (DNS)

A hierarchical, distributed database that contains mappings of DNS
domain names to various types of data, such as **Internet Protocol**
(**IP**) addresses. DNS enables the location of computers and services by
names that are user-friendly and meaningful, and it also enables the
discovery of other information stored in the **database**.

At present, the Domain Name System only recognizes domain names
consisting of a combination of **ASCII** characters, including A to Z, 0 to
9 and the hyphen '-'. These letter, number and dash characters are based
on the English writing system.

However, the **Internet** has grown from its roots as a small research
network that operated predominantly in English into a global electronic
commerce medium. Up to the present day most common Internet applications have used the ASCII character set to represent text in English.
There are now Internet users all over the world whose native language
is represented in character sets other than ASCII. These non-ASCII character sets are not supported in the global DNS. Thus the current DNS

D

does not adequately address the large population of non-English speaking Internet users.

It is now generally agreed that the global Internet community must expand the current DNS to support more than just English characters. Specifically, the desire is to internationalize names used on the web in website addresses – the Uniform Resource Locators (**URLs**). This expansion would include not only names that are very close to English, such as the German word 'straße', but also some very different from English, such as Chinese and Japanese characters and words.

Amending the current DNS to recognize non-English characters requires a system that can:

- interpret differences in written forms of communication;
- adapt to how computer systems support local written languages;
- overcome technological barriers for supporting those languages.

This is the current challenge for those working on DNS.

Dongle

A dongle is either a device allowing the computer to be locked, or hardware or software to prevent unauthorized use, usually inserted between the output port and the device or the cord connecting PC cards to external connections such as networks and phone lines.

Download

The process of taking a file (text, photo, video, sound etc.) from the Internet and placing it on the computer for future use. The use of **ADSL/broadband** has made the process of downloading large files much quicker as these systems can reduce the time required by a factor of between 10 and 20. **Uploading** is the process of sending a file from the computer to a **server** on the Internet.

D

Downloadable fonts

Downloadable fonts are a set of characters stored on disk and downloaded to a printer's memory when needed for printing a document. Downloadable fonts are most commonly used with **laser printers** and are sometimes referred to as soft fonts. By storing such fonts on disk the user is able to have access to a huge range of fonts.

Drive letter

This is the naming convention for disk drives on IBM and compatible computers. Drives are named by letter, beginning with A, followed by a colon, e.g.:

A: diskette drive
C: hard drive
D: second hard drive
E: CD/DVD drive
F: CD rewrite drive
G: zip drive (if fitted)

See Figure 13 for examples.

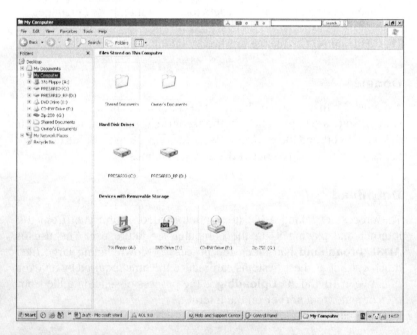

Figure 13   Drives on a typical PC with zip drive attached

Drivers

See **device drivers**.

Drives – diskette

See **diskettes**.

Drives – hard

The hard drive (or hard disk) is the computer's main media/data storage device. A hard drive consists of one or more hard disks inside air-tight casing. Most hard drives are permanently stored in a bay at the front of the computer. The disk is divided into sectors. Hard disks are a magnetic means of storage and are read and written to magnetically. Hard disks can hold huge quantities of data – modern examples of personal computers having capacities of +128 GB. Each hard disk is divided into sectors and tracks. The more tracks, the greater the capacity of the disk. The simplified example shown in Figure 14 has only 4 sectors and 5 tracks with sector 1, track 2 being illustrated. Every part of the hard disk can thus be uniquely addressed.

The disk is rotated at high speed (between 4500 and 10,000 rpm) and read by heads that move out and back across the disk. The delay in finding the required sector and track is known as rotational delay, the time taken being known as the seek time (usually less than 10 milliseconds). As time goes on, linked data can become more and more spread out over the disk and the time taken to collate all the relevant data can slow the computer down considerably. To alleviate this the user should **defragment** the hard drive periodically.

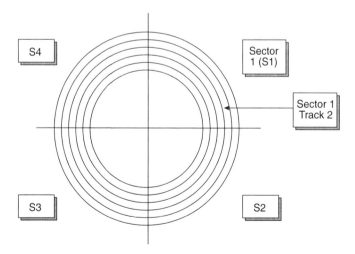

D

Figure 14   Schematic of a simplified hard disk

Duplex

The simultaneous transmission of data in both directions using two channels.

DVD/DVD(R)/DVD(RW)

A Digital Video Disk (DVD) is a type of disc drive that allows for large amounts of data on one disk the size of a standard Compact Disc (**CD**). Introduced as early as 1997 for commercial use, DVDs are now widely used for storing and viewing video and have replaced older standards such as VHS that used magnetic tapes. To play a DVD on a computer a user must have a DVD drive as well as a DVD player, which is a software program designed to play and control a DVD disk.

DVD-ROM

DVD disks with a read only memory that cannot be written to.

Dynamic disk

A dynamic disk is a physical disk that can be accessed only by Windows® 2000 and Windows® XP. Dynamic disks provide features that basic disks do not, such as support for volumes that span multiple disks. Dynamic disks use a hidden **database** to track information about dynamic volumes on the disk and other dynamic disks in the computer.

Dynamic Link Libraries (DLLs)

DLL is a type of file used with Microsoft Windows® software programs, and Windows® drivers. DLL files contain one or more executable subroutines that can be called by one or more programs. DLL files enable software developers to use Microsoft's or other companies' routines to perform common tasks and help prevent unnecessary duplication of commonly used codes. DLL files are like the dictionaries in a library. The library needs one set of dictionaries rather than a set for each group of shelves. This saves valuable space as different users (programs in the case of a computer) can access the same set of dictionaries or DLLs.

D

E-books

E-books are books that can be **downloaded** in full or in part from the Internet. They can either be read on screen or printed. They may or may not be free, usually not. E-books have not been as successful as first envisaged, due possibly to the fatigue effects on the eye of reading from a screen, the time taken to print together with the printing costs, and a cultural attachment to traditional books. E-books do allow the user to download only those parts of a book that he or she actually requires and many books can be stored on a single CD. Notwithstanding the advantages, it is perhaps easier to scan, revisit pages, move forward and contemplate a traditional book than one on screen.

E-books are often provided in **PDF (Portable Data File)** format to retain the author/publisher's layout.

E-commerce

In September 1999, UK television news services reported that the UK Prime Minister, Tony Blair, was to appoint an 'E-envoy' to promote the effective use of commercial activities carried out using the Internet. The reports quoted the fact that in 1999 there were 500,000 companies actually conducting business on the Internet, a figure that was expected to grow to a staggering 8 million by 2002 with revenue exceeding £5 billion by 2003. In the UK alone it was predicted that by the end of 2000 no fewer than 9 million Britons would have access to an Internet connection (source ITV Teletext service 12 September 1999).

Companies using the Internet for business in 2004 ranged from the major holiday companies, airlines, travel agents, book suppliers and antique houses down to a small kilt (and other Highland dress) supplier in a small town in Scotland.

In early 2000 there was a great deal of stock-market speculation in the so-called 'dot com' companies, i.e. those companies set up to conduct their operations over the Internet. Whilst the share value of many such companies initially rose rapidly, there was a serious fall in share values in April 2000, which led many commentators to believe that the growth had been too rapid. There had been complaints that the UK government was neglecting traditional industries such as shipbuilding etc. and placing too much reliance on e-commerce for the future prosperity of the country.

It has been suggested that future success will go to those managers and businesses that can function effectively and creatively in the emerging digital economy, with those who fail to grasp the opportunities being left behind. Power now belongs to customers who demand products that deliver new dimensions of value both in terms of time and of content, in addition to the more traditional price and quality values. By removing geographic constraints e-commerce can achieve just that. As a simple example, somebody living in the Highlands of Scotland may be 70–80 miles away from their nearest bookshop and yet can obtain the volumes that they require through one of the on-line bookshops such as amazon.com within 48 hours, thus saving themselves time and the cost of travel. Whilst e-commerce will never replace the social aspects of shopping, it can, and does, free up time considerably and thus adds value.

One of the most common manifestations of e-commerce is in the field of home shopping using the Internet. There is nothing new about the concept of home shopping. As the settlers poured across middle America in the nineteenth century, companies such as Sears realized that the massive distances involved in reaching the nearest department store created a market for mail-order shopping. Such companies produced mammoth catalogues containing items as diverse as clothes and farm implements. Even today many people still use a home-shopping catalogue for mail order and this is a thriving sector of the retail industry. No longer do orders have to be placed by mail and an agent used to collect payment. Modern mail order uses the telephone and facsimile technology coupled to credit card payments for those who desire a quicker and more convenient service.

US television stations pioneered the introduction of shopping channels devoted entirely to promoting products and taking orders over the telephone, a development that is now gaining ground in the UK with the introduction of cable, satellite and digital television, which allow more channels to be accessed from home. E-commerce is a natural extension of home shopping, recent developments allowing those without a computer but with a digital television to become part of the marketplace.

Given such diversity it would be impossible to mention every type of business operating on the Internet as new companies and sectors are being added continually. By 2000 one of the latest applications of e-commerce was the conducting of antique auctions by the major auction houses. No longer did a buyer need to fly from New York to London to bid for a piece or employ an agent. They could see the piece on their personal computer at home, examine its provenance and then bid electronically, and if successful pay using a credit card.

On-line banking is a major e-commerce growth area and has its own entry later in the list under **on-line banking**.

E-commerce depends for its success and growth on effective and secure means of payment – see **electronic payment of funds**, **encryption** and **Secure Electronic Transaction (SET)** in the list of definitions and concepts.

Supermarkets such as the UK market leader Tesco also offer an on-line service, something that is very useful for bulk purchases or for those in more remote areas. The delivery charge is offset by savings on both the customer's transport costs and savings made on products. The Tesco website (see Figure 15) provides details of previous purchases and delivery address etc. making it very easy to use after logging in with the customer's **password**. Many different kinds of retailers, from furniture to model railways, provide a similar service.

The European budget airline EasyJet is a totally Internet operation with all transactions being conducted via the web.

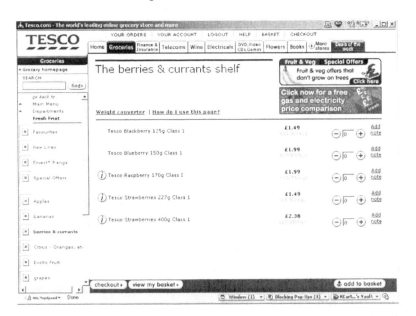

Figure 15   Part of a Tesco shopping list
Reproduced with permission of Tesco

A recent development that is connected to e-commerce is that of **on-line gambling**.

See also **loyalty cards**.

Aldrich, D. F. (1999), *Mastering the Digital Marketplace* (New York: John Wiley).
Crowder, D. A. and Crowder, R. (2000), *Shopping Online Safely* (New York: IDG).
Saunders, R. (2001), *Business the Amazon Way* (Oxford: Capstone).
Spector, R. (2000), *Amazon.com – Get Big Fast* (London: Random House).
Birch, A. and Schneider, D. (2001), *The Age of Etail* (Oxford: Capstone).
Seybold, P. (1998), *Customers.com* (New York: Random House).

EEPROM (Electrically Erasable Programmable Read-Only Memory)

EEPROM is a type of programmable **ROM (Read Only Memory)** that can be erased and reprogrammed using an electrical charge. Unlike most memory inside a computer this type of memory remembers **data** when the power is turned off and is thus non-volatile. EEPROM is often used to store information for the computer's **BIOS**.

Electromagnetic interference (EMI)

Electromagnetic interference is a type of interference that is caused by magnetic fields. These fields can cause interference in any type of electric device. An example of this is the flickering on a monitor caused by an electric fan placed near to it. The UK Computers for Schools initiative of the 1980s used computers that were loaded from audio cassette tapes. The writer was the head teacher of a school that was located next to the Dover–London railway line, an electric line worked on the third rail principle. If the computer was loading when an electric train passed, the system would crash due to the interference.

Electromagnetic pulse (EMP)

A nuclear device exploded in the atmosphere would create an electric charge that would destroy the delicate electronics of all but the most carefully shielded devices. An EMP is potentially more damaging than a ground burst. It kills few but because we have become so dependent on delicate electronic circuitry the results would be catastrophic as literally nothing – computers, aircraft, washing machines, vehicles, telephones, medical equipment etc. – would work.

Electromagnetic spectrum

The electromagnetic spectrum is a full range of radiation in nature.

E

These include radio, microwave, **infra-red**, visible, ultraviolet, x-rays and gamma-rays. Each radiation gives out a different type of energy or waves that can be detected with the proper apparatus. Our eyes can only see what is called the visible spectrum, i.e. the colours we recognize. Infra-red and ultra-violet are beyond the extremes of the visible spectrum and are thus invisible although we can experience their effects as heat if our skin is exposed to them for too long.

Electronic payment (or transfer) of funds

The transfer of monies in payment for goods and services electronically from the payee's bank or credit card account to the recipient's bank account. Such transfers require the security of **Security Electronic Transaction (SET)**.

Email (electronic mail)

Email is one of the major manifestations of the synergy gained by linking computer and telephone technology. Virtually unknown in the UK before the 1980s, email has become a normal method of business communications and has spread rapidly into the domestic market. With its ability to send document files, pictures, greetings cards etc. to anybody in the world with an Internet connection, email has meant that time and distance have been truly overcome. A message typed in London can be in the inbox of somebody in New York in seconds and at the cost of a local telephone call.

Towards the end of the twentieth century, electronic mail – email – became one of the fastest growing communication mediums in human history. As a means of communication, email came about as a combination of older, telephone technology and the widespread use of computers. The earliest email systems were dedicated internal ones serving a single organization. The growth of the Internet, however, allowed every computer user to obtain an email link with another user.

The major advantages of email are:

- The ability to send written messages in real time to a user anywhere else in the world at relatively little cost. In many cases there will only be the cost of a local telephone call or, if the user has a free-phone ISP plan, no telephone charges at all.
- The ability to send files, pictures and audio to another user.
- The ability to send a message or document to multiple users simultaneously.

E

- The ability to file received and sent material on the computer system.

Facsimile (fax) machines can send text but they are not able to attach files etc. For many purposes email has replaced both facsimile and voice telephone communications. In the UK, many of the financial problems besetting the postal service in the early years of the twenty-first century were attributed to the lowering of conventional mail volumes (often referred to as 'snail mail') due to the huge increase in the use of email

Business users of email have a fast and cost-effective method of keeping in contact with their sales force, head office and customers. Email does not depend on a recipient being at their home base to access a message. A laptop computer with a modem and a telephone point are all that are needed to make a connection. Even if these are unavailable there are Internet cafés etc. in more and more locations worldwide where, for a few dollars, Internet time can be purchased.

Many hotel rooms are being equipped with Internet-compatible telephone sockets and even modern cruise ships are fitted with 'cyber studies' so that emails can be sent and received even in the middle of the ocean. The latest generation of mobile telephones also have facilities for accessing email.

Email has a number of functions that are similar to those of a conventional mail system, albeit infinitely quicker. Just like telephone messages, emails travel at the speed of light, i.e. 186,282 miles per second (299,792,458 metres per second). However, emails are like letters and telephone connections – they need an address to which they are sent.

Email is composed and sent to the Internet via the connection that the user has set up (more than likely the user's **Internet Service Provider – ISP)**. The email address of the intended recipient (see next section) indicates the domain name to which the email should be delivered, e.g. somebody@aol.com (for a recipient using America On Line) or another.person@msn.com (for a Microsoft Network® user) etc.

Letters are addressed to name, road, town, country, postcode (or a similar variation). Emails are addressed to somebody@somewhere. The somebody is the name the person is using as their screen name. It may be their real name, part of their real name or a nickname. Depending on the email system being used, the name may be marksmith@somewhere, mark.smith@somewhere, mark_smith@somewhere or MSmith456@ somewhere (there may be more than one Mark Smith at that domain and it may be necessary to add the numbers to the name to distinguish between similarly named individuals).

E

The @ sign stands for 'at' i.e. somebody at somewhere; the somewhere is the **domain name** as discussed earlier.

Just like a postal address the email address is unique to one individual or organization or part of an organization. A company might have a
series of email addresses for customer service inquiries, product
inquiries etc., as well as addresses for specific individuals.

In summary:

- email allows businesses to send messages and other information
  quickly and cheaply over long distances;
- email can send messages to any number of recipients simultaneously;
- email can be accessed from locations other than a person's home
  base;
- pictures and audio can also be sent using email;
- email addresses are unique to the user and have the format some-
  body@somewhere;
- the sender receives a notification when a message delivery fails.

Colleagues, family and friends who are on-line can be readily contacted
and as there is no telephone bell to ring and disturb people, the problem
of time zones is eliminated. Email, despite its protocols, lacks the
personal touch but for instant messages, and indeed communications, it
is hard to beat.

Just examining an email address can provide a number of clues. For
example, .ac near the end of an address indicates that the address is at
an academic institution, .gov indicates a government body, .co is used
for companies etc. and .com is used by communication providers, with
other organizations using .org. US addresses have nothing at the end but
.uk represents Britain (the United Kingdom), .ca being Canada and so on.
Thus amazon.co.uk, the UK part of the bookseller Amazon, becomes
self-explanatory. (See **domain names**.)

Email programs are usually provided by **Internet Service Providers
(ISP)** and at their most basic contain an email inbox for incoming
messages, an email outbox for outgoing messages, email storage folders
and an email address book where email addresses can be stored and
accessed to save manual input each time a message is sent. Email provision has become more sophisticated and now also often includes anti-
spam protection, **virus** scanning of incoming mail, and remote access
so that emails can be collected and sent from other computers in **cyber
cafés** etc.

E

Embedded object

Information created in another program that has been pasted inside a document is known as an embedded object. When information is embedded it is still possible to edit the information in the new document using toolbars and menus from the original program. Embedded information is not linked to the original source. If information is changed in one place, it is not updated in the other.

Encapsulation

- In networking, encapsulation is the process of taking data from one protocol and translating it into another so that the data can continue across a network and be understood by the receiver.
- In programming, encapsulation is information within a module or other packaged section of code that enables the program or programmer to use the code while keeping it intact so other programs can use it.

Encryption

The scrambling of data to make it unintelligible to third parties during transmission. An encrypted file appears as a string of gibberish. In order to read or use the file, it must be decrypted. Files are usually encrypted using encryption programs. In most cases only users with the correct password are able to use the encryption program to make the file readable again. Encryption is of particular importance in **e-commerce**, where it is important that credit card details are encrypted to maintain security.

The art of encryption is an extremely old one with examples dating back to at least the Egyptians. Cracking codes has always been given a high priority by governments and the military. The breaking of the German Enigma code by the Allied cryptographers at Bletchley Park in the UK during the Second World War is believed to have had a strategic influence on the outcome of the conflict.

Enter key

Also known as a return key, the enter key is used to move a cursor to the next line or execute a command or operation. It is common for most standard keyboards to have two enter or return keys, one on the keyboard and another on the numeric keypad. The term **return key** is

E

derived from typewriter technology when the carriage had to be physically returned to the beginning of the next line. The enter key is usually the largest key on the keyboard and situated to the extreme right of the main qwerty keys (designed for the majority of users who are right-handed).

EPOS (Electronic Point of Sale)

EPOS works by reading **bar codes** using a **bar code reader** to assist in determining buying patterns and as an aid to stock-control. EPOS also sends the price of an item as read from the bar code to the till point. At its simplest EPOS can simply register the price of an item, whilst more complex systems can register that an item should be reordered. Supermarkets make considerable use of EPOS to ensure that they can monitor customer buying patterns and ensure that they always have adequate stocks of items.

Ergonomics

Ergonomics is the study of physical working arrangements. In terms of ICT ergonomics helps the user by ensuring that equipment is arranged so as to make it easy to use and to prevent the dangers of **RSI (repetitive strain injury)** that can occur using a badly placed keyboard. Computer use can lead to muscular, eye and mental fatigue and careful arrangement of equipment can help alleviate these problems. Peripherals, manuals, paper etc. also need to be arranged to maximize ease of use.

Error messages

Messages produced by the computer when an error has occurred within a program either through an internal problem or an illegal command. The messages provide information for both the user and the technical support staff as to the nature of the error. One of the most common Internet errors is a '404 error', indicating that a web page cannot be found. The usual cause of this error is that the **URL** has been inputted incorrectly or that the page is defunct. The error message suggests that the user checks the URL in the first instance to ensure that it is correct.

Windows® XP allows the user to send details of major failures to Microsoft via the Internet if and when they occur. This aids Microsoft in discovering any bugs in the software or any conflicts with the operating software for peripherals etc.

E

Ethernet

Originally known as Alto Aloha Network and later changed to Ethernet, Ethernet is a widely used **Local Area Network (LAN)** protocol originally created by Xerox PARC in 1973.

Spurgeon, C. (2000), *Ethernet – the Definitive Guide* (Farnham: O'Reilly UK).

.exe file

An executable file (.exe); as contrasted with a document or data file. Usually executed by double-clicking its icon or a shortcut on the desktop, or by entering the name of the program at a command prompt. Executable files can also be executed from other programs, batch files or various script files.

Expert systems

Also referred to as knowledge-based systems, expert systems are programmed using **artificial intelligence** techniques in order to provide information and decisions in particular fields of human activity, such as medical diagnosis. Although expert systems can make suggestions, the decision should remain with the user. Expert systems have been blamed for some stock-market problems because they triggered sell instructions based on small movements of price – movements that did not in fact indicate a trend. Unfortunately inordinate faith had been placed in the systems and humans did not intervene. An expert system uses reasoning based on known facts and rules to determine an answer to a question. Expert systems may employ **fuzzy logic**.

Extranet

A private network that allows controlled access to third parties such as customers and suppliers. Care needs to be taken to ensure security as each time the network is accessed externally there is the danger of attack or **hacking**. The benefit is the increased support to customers and suppliers that the extranet provides. Although a user may have access to an extranet, the extranet may only display information that he or she is privileged to see and/or only allow access to specific sections of the extranet.

E

FAQs (frequently asked questions)

A section of the help function on many websites that provides answers to those queries that have been frequently raised. The site designers hope that by providing such answers users will not need to email or telephone to have problems resolved. FAQs may be technical or may be concerned with the product and services, such as train tickets, hotel bookings, conditions of service, payment and delivery etc.

Fault tolerance

Fault tolerance is a setup or configuration that helps prevent a computer or **network** device from failing in the event of an unexpected problem or error. To make a computer or network device more fault tolerant requires that the user or company be proactive and think about the circumstances that might cause a computer or network device to crash and fail, and then to take the necessary steps to prevent the computer or network device from failing when that problem occurs. Examples of steps that can be taken are:

1. Power failure: Ensure that back-up power supplies kick in immediately the main supply fails.
2. Power surge: Provide surge protection to the system to help prevent the device from failing in the event of a power surge.
3. Data loss: Make regular backups and, in the case of large organizations ensure the storage of backed up data at a remote location.
4. Device/computer failure: Have a second device, computer and/or computer components available in the event of failure to prevent a long down time.
5. Unauthorized access: Provide **firewalls** and **password/PIN** protection.
6. Overload: set up an alternate computer or network device that can be used as an alternative access point or can share the load if the main system becomes overloaded.
7. Virus: Ensure that the computer has updated **virus** definitions so that viruses can be quarantined before causing any damage.

Favourites

See **bookmarks.**

Fax (facsimile)

Introduced as a result of developments in the Second World War, the facsimile machine matches telephone and photocopier technologies to allow documents to be sent over telephone lines. Whilst it may well be superseded by a scanner + PC + email, many businesses rely on fax to send messages quickly and conveniently. It is especially useful when complex instructions or diagrams need to be seen by somebody many miles away.

Fibre optics

Wire commonly made out of glass or plastic that carries light signals. Optical fibre cabling has an increased speed, capacity and clarity of signal compared to earlier traditional cables. Fibre optics is finding a useful place in **network**s. Data can be packaged as bursts in a similar manner to **multiplexers** thus increasing the amount of data that can be sent.

File

A portion of a software program that is used to store data, information, settings, and/or commands used with that program.

Files can be named using almost any combination of letters and numbers although the following ones constitute illegal characters and cannot be used in filenames or directories in most operating systems:

\ / : * ? " < > |

A file is created by the aid of another program. For example a user may create a text document in Word (the file will have the file extension .doc – see below) or through the MS-DOS edit command.

F

File Allocation Table (FAT)

A file system used by MS-**DOS** and other Windows®-based operating systems to organize and manage files. The file allocation table (FAT) is a data structure that Windows® creates when a volume is formatted by using one of the FATfile systems. Windows® stores information about each file in the FAT so that it can retrieve the file later.

File extensions

File extensions indicate the type of file in question and are used by the computer to identify the type of file it is dealing with. Typically two, three or four digits long, the major file extensions you are likely to come across are:

.au .aif .aiff   Macintosh sound files
.avi   Video for Windows®
.bat   Batch files
.bmp   **bitmat** graphics format. Files saved as Windows® bitmaps take up much more space than the same file saved as a **.jpg** file.
.cmd   Command (batch files)
.dll   Microsoft® **Dynamic Link Library** files
.doc   Microsoft® Word files
.exe   Program files, e.g. Word.exe is the application file for Microsoft® Word.
.gif   Graphic files, this format is often used on the **WWW**.
.hlp   Windows® help files e.g. Word.hlp
.jsp   JavaServer pages (see **Java**)
.mp3   Moving Picture Experts Group Audio Layer 3 File. MP3 files are highly compressed audio tracks, and are very popular on the Internet.
.pdf   **Portable Data Files** used to download manuals etc.
.rtf   Rich Text Format File. An alternative format to the doc file type supported by Microsoft® Word. rtf files are **ASCII** text files and include embedded formatting commands. rtf files do not contain macros and cannot be infected with a macro virus. This makes rtf files a good document format for communicating with others via email. However, some macro viruses attempt to intercept saving a file as an rtf file and instead save it as a doc file with an rtf extension. Users can catch this trick by first reading the file in a simple text editor like Notepad. doc files will be nearly unreadable, while rtf files will be readable. This file type has the extension .rtf.

F

File server

Used for **networks**, the file server is a specially configured computer fitted with a network card and enhanced memory and disk storage. Its role is to control access to shared storage, directories and files plus the exchange of files between the users of the network.

File Transfer Protocol (FTP)

FTP or File Transfer Protocol was first proposed in 1971 and developed for implementation on hosts at the Massachusetts Institute of Technology (MIT), and as such predates the World Wide Web (WWW). FTP is a standard way to transfer files between computers. The method has built-in error checking. One of the main uses of FTP is to download software. File Transfer Protocol sites on the Internet can be distinguished by ftp replacing www as a prefix.

Firewall

A firewall prevents computers on a network from communicating directly with external computer systems. A firewall typically consists of a computer that acts as a barrier through which all information passing between the networks and the external systems must travel. The firewall software analyses information passing between the two and rejects it if it does not conform to preconfigured rules. More and more **Internet Service Providers (ISPs)** are providing firewall protection as part of their **broadband** access.

Firewire interface

Developed by Apple, Firewire enables hot-swappable connection of digital products such as cameras and camcorders to a personal computer. Also referred to as IEEE or **Sony iLink**.

F

Flash

Shorthand term for Macromedia Flash, Flash was originally known as 'Future Splash Animator'. Macromedia Flash is a software program that allows users to create animated works that can be easily viewable over the Internet using a (usually free) Macromedia Flash **plug-in**.

Flash memory

Flash memory is a type of computer memory developed by the Intel Corporation in the USA. Flash memory is non-volatile memory (that is an integrated circuit that does not need continuous power to retain the data). It is much more expensive than magnetic storage and is therefore not practical as a replacement for current **hard disks** or **diskettes**.

Floppy disk

See **diskette**.

Folder

A folder is a container for programs and files in graphical user interfaces, symbolized on the screen by a graphical image (**icon**) of a file folder. A folder is a means of organizing programs and documents on a disk and can hold both files and additional folders (see Figure 16).

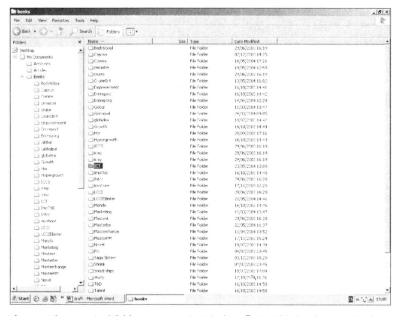

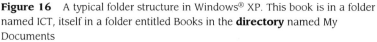

Figure 16   A typical folder structure in Windows® XP. This book is in a folder named ICT, itself in a folder entitled Books in the **directory** named My Documents

Footprint

The footprint is a measure of the physical space on a desk or in a room that a computer system takes up.

Frames

A frame is a movable or non-movable portion of a web page to help make the navigation easier. Frames allow information to be stored logically and separately on a web page (see Figure 17).

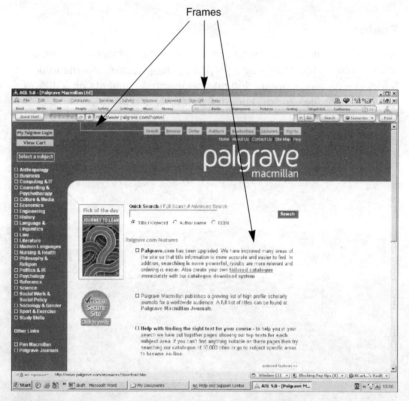

Figure 17   Some of the frames on the Palgrave Macmillan website

Fuzzy logic

A feature of **expert systems** that allows a degree of uncertainty to be built in to the logical deduction process. Conclusions come with a probability value indicating the chance that the probability is correct. Used by a computer program where an answer does not need to be absolutely true or false, fuzzy logic is commonly used in **artificial intelligence**, where the system may need to respond to something it may not absolutely know, or know only part of. To this extent the human experience is a model as we rarely have all the information needed to hand and work on the basis of probability. Generally fuzzy logic is achieved by defining several rules and having the program perform a function by following those set rules.

F

Gg

Games

See **Applications/software – games.**

Gateway

A gateway is used to connect two **Local Area Networks (LAN)** of different types (cf. **Bridge**).

GIF

Pronounced 'jiff' and short for Graphic Interchange Format, GIF is a file extension and a type of bitmapped graphics file used primary for graphic files on the Internet.

Globalization

The integration of the global economy, involving the dismantling of trade barriers and the expanding political and economic power of multinational corporations. ICT has aided the growth of globalization by providing efficient real-time communications including the transmission of documents and **videoconferencing**. This facilitates the process of running commercial operations at considerable distance.

ICT innovations have contributed to globalization by supplying the infrastructure and means for transglobal world connections and networks. In particular, developments in means of transport, communications and data processing have allowed global links to become denser, faster, more reliable and much cheaper. Physical transport is as important as the Internet. Large-scale and rapid globalization has depended on a host of innovations relating to coaxial and later fibre-optic cables, jet engines, packaging and preservation techniques, semiconductor devices, computer software, and so on. In other words, global relationships could not develop without physical tools to effect panglobal contacts.

The global acceptability of credit/debit cards and technological developments now mean that, thanks to the Internet, any business, of any size, anywhere, can become global.

Google

See **search engine.**

Gopher

An early means of web navigation, Gopher was developed in 1991 and first used at the University of Minnesota and named after its mascot, a small US mammal known as a gopher. Gopher is a menu-driven interface that allows a user to browse for text information served off various Gopher servers. Later versions of Gopher such as HyperGopher allowed users also to view **GIF** and **JPEG** files. After 1996 most Gopher servers were either converted to the **World Wide Web** or taken off-line.

GPS (Global Positioning Satellite)

GPS (or **Satnav – satellite navigation**) equipment uses **satellites** to plot an extremely accurate position on the earth's surface using software that compares the signals from the satellites. Originally a military application, GPS can be used with hand-held computers and embedded systems on small boats, motor cars and even for hill walkers etc. to provide a very accurate navigation system at relatively low cost. GPS software can be loaded onto a Personal Digital Assistant (**PDA**) that can make the PDA into a dual-function device (provided that a receiver is attached) as it can be used for navigation whilst in a vehicle or when out walking without losing its computer applicability.

See also **satellites.**

Graphics applications

See **applications/software – graphics.**

G

Graphics tablet

A graphics tablet, together with its associated pressure pen and software, enables a user to produce handwritten notes and annotations including drawings onto the screen. The user is able to annotate documents etc. and then save both the original and the annotation.

GUI (Graphical User Interface)

Pronounced 'gooey', a GUI uses graphical representations that are selected by the user. Small pictures or **icons** are displayed, for example a **diskette**, and when the user clicks on this icon the screen displays the contents of the A: (3.5-inch diskette) drive. Many programs such as Word® use GUI for the various toolbars, providing a graphical and/or written description of what the icon controls (see Figure 18).

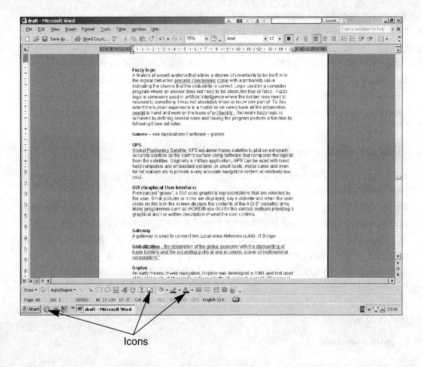

Icons

Figure 18 A GUI (Graphical User Interface) screen

G

Hacking and hackers

Hackers are individuals who illegally break into other computer systems to damage and/or steal information. Some hackers may not have malign intent and break in just to prove that they can do so. Such individuals often leave a flag or message on the hacked computer system to show that they have penetrated security.

Hacking is of international concern. Whilst some hackers may claim to be benign, there is always the danger either that terrorists will disrupt military, political and economic systems or that fraud will be committed by criminal elements. Those involved in industrial or political/military espionage often use hacking to exploit the mine of data and information that can be found stored on computer systems. Individuals are also at risk from hacking, especially if they use **e-commerce** and **Internet banking**.

The Internet has made hacking an international problem and governments routinely cooperate to prosecute those of their citizens who hack into foreign computer systems.

Many of the so-called benign hackers are youngsters who have considerable computer skills but choose to use them inappropriately and without thought to the grave consequences that any disruption may cause. In the vast majority of the world's jurisdictions hacking is a serious criminal offence.

Commercial and official computer users need to take considerable care to have adequate security (**firewalls** etc.) in place together with **passwords** and **encryption** to protect their systems.

Half duplex

Data transmission that occurs in both directions but not simultaneously as with **duplex**.

Hard copy

A paper copy of a document prepared electronically. Computers were supposed to lead to the paperless office but this has not occurred in practice, as many users still prefer to have a paper copy of a document to annotate or for secure storage. There have been concerns that far from saving paper ICT is adding to the increased deforestation of the earth because of the ease with which messages can be sent and the numbers of hard copies that are taken of them. At one time a single memo might be passed around 10 people. Today each receives an email and each makes a copy – the result is a 10-fold increase in paper usage!

Hard disk

See **drives – hard.**

Hardware

The physical components of a computer system, including any peripheral equipment such as printers, modems and mouse devices, are referred to as hardware – in contrast to the programs used by the computer, which are known as software.

Hardware configuration

The hardware configuration is the resource settings that have been allocated for a specific device. Each device on a computer has a hardware configuration. Some of the configuration settings can be changed to suit the user. An example of this are the buttons on a mouse that can be swapped around electronically to suit a left-handed user.

Hardware profile

This is data that describes the configuration and characteristics of specific computer equipment. This data can be used to configure computers for using peripheral devices.

Help

In the early days of home and small business computing every computer and piece of software seemed to come with huge paper manuals filled with information that the user rarely needed. The modern approach is to equip software with a help function that allows the user to input key words or search an on-screen index for assistance with a particular topic (see Figure 19). Major software providers also provide Internet help on-

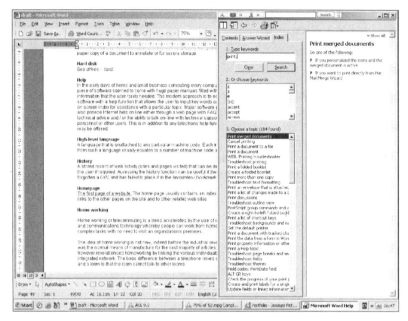

Figure 19 The help function for Word®

line, either through a web page with **FAQs** and technical advice and/or the ability to talk on-line with technical support personnel or other users. This is in addition to any telephone help function that may be offered.

On-line help refers to help pages that are located on web pages and are accessed over the Internet

See **on-line help.**

Hibernation

As in nature, hibernation is a state in which a computer shuts down (usually after a time specified by the user) after saving everything in memory onto the hard disk. When the computer is brought out of hibernation, all programs and documents that were open are restored to the desktop. Hibernation is a much deeper state than standby. In Windows® hibernation is set through the power options in **control panel**.

High-level language

A language that is unattached to any particular machine code. Each instruction from such a language usually equates to a number of machine code instructions.

History

A stored record of web activity (sites and pages visited) that can be deleted by the user if required. Accessing the history function can be useful if the user has forgotten a **URL** and has failed to place it in the **favourites/bookmark** function.

The user can instruct the **browser** as to how long items should be kept in the history folder. **Internet Explorer** allows items to be kept between 0 and 999 days.

Hive

A section of the registry that appears as a file on the hard disk. The registry sub-tree is divided into hives (so called because of their resemblance to the cellular structure of a beehive). A hive is a discrete body of keys, sub-keys and values that is rooted at the top of the registry hierarchy. A hive is backed by a single file and a .log file, which are in the systemroot\System32\Config or the systemroot\Profiles\username folders.

By default, most hive files (Default, SAM, Security and System) are stored in the systemroot\System32\Config folder. The systemroot\Profiles folder contains the user profile for each user of the computer. Because a hive is a file, it can be moved from one system to another, although to edit any part of it the Registry Editor must be employed.

Home working

Home working or telecommuting is a trend accelerated by the use of Information and Communications Technology whereby people can work from home on complex tasks with no need to visit an organization's premises.

The idea of home working is not new, indeed before the Industrial Revolution it was the normal means of manufacture for the vast majority of articles. ICT has, however, revolutionized home working by linking the various individuals into an integrated network. The basic difference between a telephone-linked computer and a loom is that the loom cannot talk to other looms.

Home working can have psychological disadvantages. Work is a social activity and those working from home on a permanent basis can become detached and lonely. It is imperative that organizations employing ICT-based home workers ensure that there is some degree of human contact, even if it is only by telephone. **Telecottages** have evolved to help overcome this problem.

The advantages of homeworking are:

For the organization,
- removal of the need for costly premises;
- staff efficiency unaffected by the rigours of travel to and from work;
- flexible deployment of staff.

For the individual,
- flexible working;
- no, or less, home-to-work travel;
- no need to move home to be near the job.

The recent trend for call centres to be located in countries other than those served by the organization, for example, British financial institutions with their call centres in India, is a logical extension of the homeworking concept. Information and Communication Technolgy allows the worker and the organization to be physically separate without impairing efficiency.

Homepage

The first page of a website. The homepage usually contains an index and Hypertext Markup Language (**HTML**) links to the other pages on the site and to other related websites (see Figure 20).

Host

A Windows® computer that runs a server program or service used by network or remote clients is known as a host. Many websites, especially those operated by individuals and small businesses, are run on host **servers** provided by third parties.

H

Host name

The **Domain Name System** name of a device on a network. These names are used to locate computers on the network. To find another computer, its host name must either appear in the Hosts file or be known by a DNS **server**. For most Windows® computers, the host name and the computer name are the same.

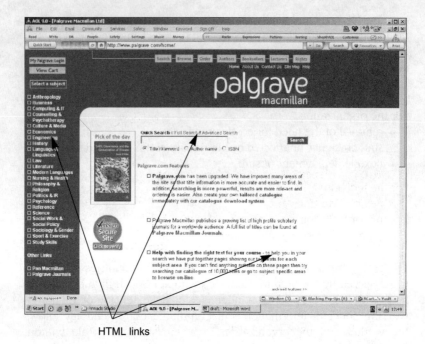

HTML links

Figure 20 The Palgrave Macmillan homepage

Hot desking

An arrangement in some organizations where offices have been reorganized as a result of ICT developments. Instead of a dedicated desk or work space, those staff who do not need to have a permanent desk in the office because they are on the road etc. are provided with a laptop and modem so that they can work from any location that has telephone access. When they do need to return to base they can use a work space that is available to all staff. Such a hot desking (as it is known) approach also requires that worktop spaces be kept free of any personal items.

Hotmail

Hotmail from Microsoft® is the world's largest provider of free, web-based email. With Hotmail, users can read and receive email messages from any computer in the world that has an Internet connection and a web browser that supports graphics, such as Microsoft® Internet Explorer 4.0 or later, or Netscape Navigator 4.08 or later. Hotmail is useful for people who use more than one computer, travel frequently, or do not own a computer. Messages are stored in a central server, ensuring that the user's inbox is always up to date, no matter where he or she is.

Basic Hotmail is for email only and does not support web browsing and searching.

HTML (Hypertext Markup Language)

HTML is a language used to create electronic documents, especially pages on the World Wide Web, that contain connections called hyperlinks to other pages.

HTML or HTM is also a computer **file extension** for HTML documents.

HTTP (Hypertext Transfer Protocol)

HTTP is a set of standards that let users of the World Wide Web exchange information found on web pages. When a user wishes to access a web page it is commonly required that http:// be placed before the address allowing the browser to know it is going through HTTP. Many Internet browsers allow users the ability to specify the domain e.g. www.thisbook.com and then default to HTTP, e.g. http://www.thisbook.com

HTTPS (Hypertext Transfer Protocol over Secure Socket Layer)

HTTPS is a secure method of accessing web-page information and/or sending information across a web page. HTTPS pages display a padlock icon at the bottom right-hand corner of the page to indicate that the user is linked to a secure site.

H

Hub

A device with multiple ports that allows a number of devices to be connected to a central unit or **Local Area Network (LAN)** cable. A **USB hub** can be connected to a **USB** port on a computer to allow a number of **plug and play** peripherals to be connected. Thus the one or two USB ports on an older machine can support a number of peripher-

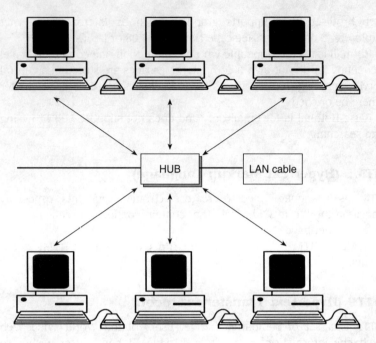

Figure 21   Use of a hub with a LAN

als without having to unplug one to make a port available (see Figure 21).

Hyperlinks

A hyperlink is an icon, graphic or word in a document or web page that links to another file or object. The World Wide Web is composed of hyperlinks linking millions of pages and files to one another. Hyperlinks are either **icons**/graphics or underlined (and often coloured) words where the screen pointer changes to a right hand with the digit finger

Figure 22   Change of pointer on hyperlinks

Some of this page's hyperlinks

Figure 23   Part of a web page containing hyperlinks: a left click on the bottom hyperlink calls up the relevant page (see Figure 24)

extended when the pointer is placed over the Hyperlink (see Figure 22). A left click on the mouse etc. then directs the computer to the page referred to by the link. The use of hyperlinks enables quick and easy web navigation without the need to be constantly typing in **URLs**. Hyperlinks can be inserted into normal documents such as those produced by Word® and which are stored on the computer. Provided that there is an open link to the Internet, clicking on the link will take the user to the relevant web page. In Word® hyperlinks are inserted and removed via the 'insert' command button. (See Figures 23 and 24 for examples of hyperlinks.)

H

Hypertext

Text that contains **hyperlinks**.

Figure 24 The page reached from the link on Figure 23: this page is on a totally different site and contains its own frames, hyperlinks etc. (with one click the user has saved having to write in a whole URL)

H

Icon

A small image displayed on the screen to represent an object that can be manipulated by the user. Icons serve as visual mnemonics and allow the user to control certain computer actions without having to remember commands or type them at the keyboard. Icons form an important part of the **WIMP (Windows, Icons, Menus, Pointer)** concept that has made running computer applications so simple that no technical knowledge is required by the user (see Figure 25, which shows icons displayed in Microsoft Word®).

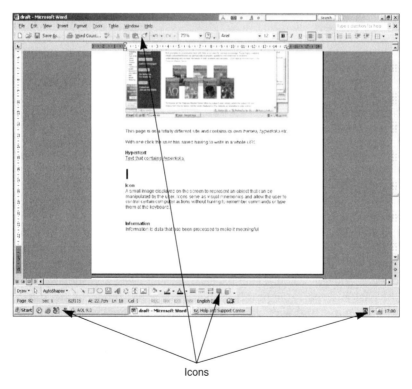

Icons

Figure 25 Icons

ICT

See **Information and Communication Technology (ICT)**.

Imaginary numbers

See **real numbers.**

IMAP (Internet Message Access Protocol)

IMAP was developed at Stanford University in the USA in 1986 and is a protocol retrieving email messages.

Infoimaging

The combination of imaging science such as **digital cameras** and **scanners** with computers and telephone technologies. The resulting images can then be manipulated, stored and transmitted.

Information

Information is **data** that has been processed to make it meaningful. Information is the output from processed data.

See also **data.**

Information and Communication Technology (ICT)

ICT refers to the technology related to the connection of computer and communication's technology to produce a **synergy** between them. ICT was originally known as IT (Information Technology). However, more and more computer-type applications also involve communication with other computers or communication devices, hence the adoption of the acronym ICT.

The power of ICT lies less in the various components but in their linkage through a **network**. Whilst the abilities of computers, tele-phones and television technologies have increased considerably over the past few years, the power of their linkage has produced the **information superhighway** whose growth has been almost exponential.

Information and Communication Technology (ICT) strategy

See **strategy (ICT).**

Information overload

Information overload is the result of having so much information that it is difficult to sort out the important from the trivial and the urgent from the less urgent. Modern technology has made this a major problem. Whilst computers can store and process information very quickly, the human brain requires more time. Even an average computer can experience information overload, especially with programmes and images that take up considerable space. It is noteworthy that the capacity of peripheral storage devices such as **diskettes**, **ZIP disks**, **CDs** etc. has grown considerably to accommodate every increasing additional storage need. Whilst a 1.44 MB diskette was the standard portable storage device for the majority of users in the 1990s, 750 MB CD and zip drives are now commonplace even in domestic situations.

The importance of information overload lies in the fact that having access to information is often useless unless it is accompanied by the ability to use the information quickly and efficiently. Extravagant use of email has led to people receiving more information than they either need or can cope with. There have been cases of people receiving email from those whose desks are in an adjacent position. The use of mailing lists and **address books** has made the sending of messages so easy that too many are probably sent to too many people, leading to time being spent opening messages that may have little relevance to the recipient. It is these kinds of actions that can lead to information overload.

Information superhighway

A term introduced by US Vice-President Al Gore during a speech on 11 January 1994 to describe a future of computers accessing and communicating over a worldwide network. This is precisely what the Internet has become – a highway along which data flows at ever-increasing speed and in ever-increasing amounts.

Infra-red (IR)

A method of transferring data without the use of wires using light from beyond the red end of the visible spectrum falling upon an infra-red-sensitive receiver. A common example of an infra-red device is a TV (or similar device) remote control. However, infra-red is also used with computers with devices such as a wireless keyboard or mouse. Unlike **Bluetooth** wireless technology, infra-red only operates on line of sight and cannot pass through obstacles, as every user of a TV remote control knows. The peripherals need to be fairly close to the receiver in order for the infra-red system to work effectively.

Infra-red port

An optical port on a computer that enables communication with other computers or devices by using infra-red light, without cables. Infra-red ports can be found on some portable computers, printers and cameras. The port needs line of sight to the device and is often hinged so that its angle can be altered.

Input devices

Peripheral devices such as a **keyboard**, a **mouse**, a **graphics tablet**, **trackerball**, microphone, **touchscreen** that allow the user to input data and commands to the computer.

Input/Output Controller (IOC)

Also known as an input/output interface or PIOC for Peripheral Input/Output Controller. The input/output controller is a device that interfaces between an input or output device and the computer or hardware device. The input/output controller on computers is commonly located on the **motherboard**. However, an I/O controller can also be an internal add-on that can be used either as a replacement or to allow for additional input or output devices for the computer.

Input/Output (I/O) port

An Input/Output (I/O) port is a channel through which data is transferred between a device and the computer. The port appears to the computer as one or more memory addresses that it can use to send or receive data.

Install

Installing is the process of either adding a new device and its drivers to the hardware or loading in new software. Installation **wizards** are employed to guide the user through the process. A screen display usually provides an indication of the progress of the installation. Most wizards allow for automatic installation plus a manual override for the user who wishes to deviate from the basic procedure.

Integers

Integers are whole numbers without any decimal points, e.g. 1, 2, 3, 4, 5 etc.

Integrated circuit

First developed in 1958 by Jack Kilby and Robert Noyce, an integrated circuit is a package containing many circuits, pathways, **transistors** and other electronic components all working together to perform a particular function or a series of functions. Integrated circuits are the foundations of computer hardware.

Technology has allowed more and more components to be placed on very tiny chips. **Large-Scale Integration** is a chip that contains between 100 and 5000 circuit elements. **Very-Large Scale Integration (VLSI)** is an integrated circuit design that contains 5000 to 50,000 components on a single chip.

Ultra-Large Scale Integration (ULSI) is an integrated circuit with more than one million components per chip. One million components on a single chip is a huge feat of miniaturization.

The process of integration that allows for smaller and smaller integrated circuits greatly aids the development of **embedded computers** and **smart cards**.

Intelligent systems

See **expert systems**.

Internet

The Internet is an open interconnection of computer networks that enables the computers and the programs they run to communicate directly. The term Internet is usually applied to the global, publicly accessible network, called simply the Internet or Net. By 2000, over 100,000 networks and 100 million users were connected via the Internet, with the number of users growing daily.

Kent, P. and Young, R. (2002), *The Complete Idiot's Guide to the Internet* (Harlow: Pearson Education).

Internet banking

See **on-line banking**.

Internet Content Rating Association (ICRA)

The Internet Content Rating Association is an international, independent organization that empowers the public, especially parents, to make informed decisions about electronic media by means of the open and objective labelling of content. ICRA's aims are to:

- protect children from potentially harmful material; and
- to protect free speech on the Internet.

The system works as follows. Web authors fill in an on-line questionnaire describing the content of their site, simply in terms of what is and is not present. ICRA then generates a Content Label (a short piece of computer code) that the author adds to his/her site. Users, especially parents of young children, can then set their Internet browser to allow or disallow access to websites based on the objective information declared in the label and the preferences of the user. The ICRA system can be used with Microsoft's® **Internet Explorer** immediately, with wider applications under development. The existing Recreational Software Advisory Council (RSAC) labels can continue to be used in both Internet Explorer and Netscape Navigator but will be phased out over time. ICRA's forerunner, the Recreational Software Advisory Council (RSAC) was involved in the development of the standard, created by the World Wide Web Consortium.

Internet Explorer

Often abbreviated as IE, Internet Explorer is Microsoft's web browser. Like Netscape Navigator, Internet Explorer enables the user to view web pages. Internet Explorer supports **Java**, **JavaScript** and **ActiveX**. Internet Explorer is included as part of the Windows® operating system and is the most frequently used web browser, having a huge market share. The packaging of Internet Explorer with Windows® and the monopoly on browsing that this has given Microsoft has been the subject of a number of court cases in both the USA and the European Union.

Internet Message Access Protocol (IMAP)

Developed at Stanford University in 1986, Internet Message Access Protocol is a **protocol** retrieving email messages. It is similar to **POP (Post Office Protocol)** but supports some additional features. For example, it allows the user to search **email** messages for **keywords** whilst the messages are still on mail server.

See also **Post Office Protocol (POP)**.

Internet – minimum hardware requirements

At the time of writing the minimum specification for accessing the Internet using a modem attached to a stand-alone computer was:

- A telephone line preferably dedicated to accessing the Internet. (Many users will already have a telephone line installed, but a dedicated Internet line means that the user is not monopolising a line required by others for telephone use).
- A 56 kBps **modem**, either external or internal. The specification of the internal modem (if fitted) can be shown by opening Control Panel in Windows® and then clicking on Modems. This will indicate the type and specification of the internal modem. A modem is required to convert **digital** signals to **analogue** and then back to digital. Achieving the maximum speed from the modem requires the telephone line to be at 100 per cent efficiency – something that rarely occurs due to **noise**.
- A computer with at least 32 MB of **RAM (Random Access Memory)**. Clicking on the system icon in Control Panel will bring up data on the computer system including RAM capacity.
- A hard drive that can store a minimum of 1 gigabyte although 2+ gigabytes are preferable. The greater the storage capacity of the hard disk, the greater the amount of material that can be **downloaded** from the Internet. Material downloaded from the Internet, especially sound and graphics, can take up a considerable amount of computer memory, hence the need for as much memory on the hard disk as possible.
- A minimum of 800 × 600 graphics colour display. The graphics capability of the machine can be found by clicking on the display icon in control panel. The higher the definition the better the picture. The graphics capability is shown by the number of **pixels**. An 800 × 600 display can accommodate 480,000 pixels, i.e. nearly half a million. The more pixels, the better the resolution of a picture.
- A **CD** drive (preferred). It is possible to subscribe to an **Internet Service Provider (ISP)** by directly downloading from the Internet. This, of course, requires that the computer be connected to the Internet. The first time the user requires to connect the system it will be necessary to use the software provided by the ISP on a compact disk. Many computers with Windows® come with the initial connections to MSN® (Microsoft Network) already in place.

A CD drive (often a combined CD/DVD drive in the most modern systems) is a necessity for most users as much of the software available commercially comes on CD. Downloading software from the Internet can take considerable time and incur high telephone costs.

- An account with an **ISP**.
- **Virus** protection.

Internet Relay Chat (IRC)

Internet Relay Chat is one of the most popular and most interactive services on the Internet. IRC can be thought of as the Internet's equivalent of Citizen's Band (CB) radio. But unlike CB, Internet Relay Chat lets people all over the world participate in real-time conversations. Using an IRC client (program) a user can exchange text messages interactively with other people all over the world. Such programs include mIRC, Pirch and Virc for Windows® and Homer or Ircle for Macintosh computers. What program is used does not really matter; all of them connect to the same chat networks. When logged into a chat session, the user converses by typing messages that are instantly sent to other chat participants. IRC has been a mechanism for transmitting **worms**.

Internet Protocol (IP) addresses

Whilst human beings use words more than numbers in everyday conversations, computers operate on a numerical basis. Every computer that is connected to the Internet has its own unique numerical address. This IP (Internet Protocol) address consists of four sets of numbers separated by dots, e.g.: 376.951.447.89. The computer has an IP address assigned to it when it is logged onto the Internet. It may not always be the same number as the last few digits can be dynamically / server allocated. It is these IP numbers that the routing mechanism of the Internet uses as addresses.

The act of typing in and sending the name of a website also sends a signal containing the user's IP address via the Internet connection to the nearest routing server. The server looks down its list of information for the IP address associated with the website name, replaces it with the IP address number, and then connects the user to the website. Messages can now flow freely both ways between the user's computer and the website.

Every Internet-connected computer has a complicated IP address but users do not have to know or remember this number as the computer does this for them. The **domain name** is a word alias for the numerical IP address.

Users and/or companies who need to register an IP address or a valid range of IP addresses must register that IP address through InterNIC.

Internet Service Provider

See ISP (Internet Service Provider).

Internet-specific companies

These are companies set up specifically to exploit the capabilities of the Internet. They fall into two categories. Firstly there are those companies that are using the Internet as their prime method of trading (e-commerce), of which amazon.com is one of the best-known examples. The second category consists of companies that provide Internet service and includes the ISPs and search engine providers. More and more companies are becoming increasingly reliant on the Internet for their commercial activities and offer discounts for e-commerce. EasyJet, the budget airline, charge a premium for telephone bookings – the vast majority of the company's business is conducted electronically on-line.

The reliance on e-commerce by these companies means that they need close collaboration with credit/debit card providers and a secure means of conducting monetary transactions. These issues are covered under **Secure Electronic Transaction (SET)** and **secure servers**.

Interpreters

An interpreter is a program that executes instructions written in a high-level language. There are two ways to run programs written in a high-level language. The most common is to use a **compiler** for the program; the other method is to pass the program through an interpreter.

An interpreter translates high-level instructions into an intermediate form, which it then executes. This is in contrast to compiling, where high-level instructions are translated directly into **machine language**. Compiled programs generally run faster than interpreted programs. The advantage of an interpreter is that it does not need to go through the compilation stage during which machine instructions are generated. This process can be time-consuming for long programs. The interpreter, however, is able to execute high-level programs immediately. This ability is often used during the development of a program, when a programmer wants to add small sections at a time and test them quickly. Interpreters are also often used in education because they allow students to program interactively.

Iomega Jaz

An Iomega® Jaz disk contains two platters and can hold I GB (2 GB with compression) of data. This data can be accessed with a seek speed of 10–12 ms thus giving it comparability to a hard disk. Whether located internally or externally the Jaz system requires connection to an **SCSI** controller. Jaz is a highly effective means of data backup due to its high speed and capacity.

Iomega Zip

An Iomega® Zip disk requires its own dedicated Iomega® Zip drive but can hold far more data than a standard **diskette**. A magnetic form of media, the single platter disks are not that much larger than standard diskettes and are read and written to in exactly the same way, making data transfer easy. Originally designed for 100 MB, then 250 MB and latterly 750 MB, the disks are extremely useful for backing up documents etc. in a speedy and effective manner. The downside is the need for a special, albeit portable, ZIP drive in order to use the Iomega® Zip system. The Zip drive is much slower than **CD** or the hard disk, typically around four times slower, unlike a **Jaz** drive.

iPod

The slim iPod is the most modern type of a digital music player. With a weight of less than two CDs, it can hold up to 3750 songs on a 15 GB model and downloads music very quickly.

iPods support the most popular audio formats, including **MP3** (up to 320 kBps), MP3 Variable Bit Rate (VBR) and WAV giving you access to a wide range of audio file types. And iPod is the only portable digital music player that supports the AAC format (Mac-only), which features CD-quality audio in smaller file sizes than MP3, so that even more songs fit on your iPod.

The latest iPods allow the user to maintaining contact lists, and have a calendar function and simple games. The iPod was designed for listening to digital music away a computer. One simple connection through a dock links the iPod to the user's PC.

ISDN (Integrated Services Digital Network)

ISDN is a telecommunications network that allows for digital voice, video and data transmission. ISDN is a broadband Internet solution that offers up to 128 kBps of data transfer. ISDN is rapidly being replaced by **ADSL/broadband** with its far greater capacity for data transfer.

ISP (Internet Service Provider)

These companies provide the link between Internet users and the World Wide Web, usually by subscription to their services. AOL (America On Line), Freeserve, BTnet, Tesconet are some well-known examples. ISPs charge either on a 'time used' basis, with the subscriber paying for the actual time used, or by flat fee – unlimited access arrangements. Where ISPs offer a free service, the subscriber usually has to pay for the cost of the (usually local) telephone call. ISPs offer access through the conventional telephone network, **broadband** or **WAP**-equipped mobile telephones.

An ISP acts as the link and gateway connecting a user to the **Internet**. The physical link between the user and the ISP is normally either a telephone line or through cable networks that also supply television and telephone facilities. Current developments include the use of **broadband** Internet access using **ADSL**, cable, wireless and even satellite technology to increase the speed of connection up to 10 times that obtained when using a telephone line.

The three basic ways that ISPs make money are by:

- free ISPs that charge for the telephone call (pay as you go);
- unmetered ISPs that charge a fixed fee (usually monthly) and use a freephone number;
- pay ISPs that charge both a subscription fee and for telephone access.

Many ISPs have different access deals depending on the degree of use that the customer makes of the Internet.

For light users the pay-as-you-go option is best for them especially if the ISP provides a local-rate telephone number.

The moderate user should look for a pricing arrangement that allows for unmetered access at non-peak times. The ISP often charges less for such an arrangement than unmetered access at any time.

The heavy user of the Internet will find that unmetered unrestricted access may provide the best option. Knowing the exact monthly cost of Internet access allows for easy budgeting.

Constant users of the Internet tend to be those who use it as part of their business activities. They may wish to be connected permanently to the Internet through a dedicated telephone or **broadband link**. **ADSL (Asymmetric Digital Subscriber Line)** allows the line to be used for telephone calls even when connected to the Internet. An unmetered arrangement is a necessity for the constant user. More and more domestic users are switching to broadband and it is expected that most of the UK will have broadband access by the end of 2004.

Many ISPs offer all of the above arrangements. Potential users should examine the various pricing packages on offer before entering into a contractual arrangement with the chosen ISP. No matter which ISP is chosen the user will have to pay for access to the Internet in some form or another – either directly to the ISP or to their telephone company. The key factors that should be borne in mind are:

1. What is the likely pattern of Internet use; will it be light, medium, heavy or constant (see above)? This will determine the optimum pricing arrangement.
2. What is the quality of the ISP's connection service? Can the user obtain a dial-up connection with ease and is the speed of access to the ISP site adequate?
3. What hclp arrangements are in place? Ideally there should be both email and telephone help arrangements. Many ISPs use a premium-rate telephone number for their help desk. The help should be available for a considerable period each day and not restricted to business hours.

One might expect an Internet Service Provider with the name AOL to do well and grow in the USA but what about the rest of the world? Why should people in, say, the UK decide to sign up with an ISP that is obviously foreign? The only reason anybody does something like that is because they receive value for money and excellent service.

When AOL was started in 1985 the number of users of personal computers was very small but growing. By 2001 it was difficult to find a home in any developed country whose members did not have access to a PC either at home or at work or increasingly both and who had not experienced the Internet. AOL alone has 30 million plus users of its branded AOL services.

For those at the cutting edge of the computer revolution it was becoming clear as early as the mid-1980s that the real growth area in usage would be the synergy of linked computers to pass information – the ICT concept that this book is designed to facilitate. In1985 Steve Case and Jim Kinnsey set up a company, Quantum Computer Services, to deliver on-line information via computer **modems**. Steve Case set up a contest for a new name for the company in 1989 and promptly won it himself with the name America On Line (AOL). AOL offered information, games and – what was a new service for the public – **email**, with the possibility to communicate with other members electronically. Email had been around in a commercial setting throughout the latter part of the 1980s but mainly as corporate networks with few means of communicating outside the corporate boundaries. Now it was becoming available in the public domain.

AOL's marketing was highly successful. AOL began the concept of giving away their software, attaching it to the covers of computer magazines and even through mailshots. The company was the first, in 1993, to offer a version of their software that ran on the Microsoft Windows® platform that was fast becoming the global norm. By 1994 there were one million AOL members and the company linked them to the Internet for the first time using aol.com. The Initial Public Offering (IPO, the first time the public are able to buy shares in a company) for AOL was in 1992 and in 1995/96 the company expanded abroad, launching AOL in the UK, Germany and Canada with local news etc. covered on its sites.

CompuServe, a competitor ISP, was acquired in 1998, the year in which AOL actually carried more messages than the US Postal Service, a testament to the manner in which email was becoming an accepted mode for communication. The power and strength of email as a global communication medium was by now growing rapidly, having moved from the purely commercial into the domestic market as well. The innovative ICQ operation, allowing users to let others know when they are on-line plus the provision of chat facilities, was also acquired that year. By 1999 ICQ had tripled its number of members since acquisition to 40 million in only 14 months. Netscape (the Internet browser) was just one of a number of brands to come under the AOL banner in 1999, the year in which AOL Hong Kong was launched.

By 2000, having expanded into Latin America (AOL Mexico and AOL Argentina), there were 27 million global AOL users with a new one joining the service every six seconds. In a major development AOL merged with Time Warner, the entertainment and media group on 11 January, 2001. Time's ancestry goes back to 1922 whilst that of Warner Brothers stretches back to 1918, the end of the First World War. The synergy between publishing, music, movies and the Internet is a powerful one. By the time of the merger the number of AOL members was approaching 30 million and the company was operating in 16 countries and in eight different languages. Having developed a strategic alliance with Sun Microsystems, AOL was a major force in the global communication arena.

Constantly being updated, the AOL products have met the needs of users across the globe despite the nationalistic nature of the name. Growth has been steady and always such as to build on synergy. Simultaneously AOL has grown by developing new products (organic growth), by acquisitions and by geographic growth to provide a one-stop solution for the Internet needs of its growing number of members.

In the eight years between the IPO and 2000, AOL stock appreciated by almost 69,000 per cent. The market valuation of AOL in 2000 was greater than that of all the publicly traded US newspaper industry, evidence of how important the Internet and its associated products has become.

Stauffer (2000) provides ample evidence in the form of quotes to suggest that there have been those who did not believe that AOL would be a success – at one time it was doubted whether it could outperform CompuServe. However, AOL is a company that has been prepared to meet challenges. By providing for a user's entire Internet needs (if he or she so wishes) within an easy-to-use framework, AOL inspires customer loyalty. The regularity by which the necessary upgrades are sent to the user and imaginative pricing schemes to suit national conditions also engender loyalty. For example, in the UK one can choose a series of pricing plans; and there is a free phone access number. Each price plan is flat rate (so unlimited time online), and uncapped, so there are no restrictions on the amount you download each month.

In 2001 in the USA, AOL experimented with providing the PC with which to access the Internet. CompuServe users in the USA have been offered a free PC following a deal with eMachines. Whilst users in other countries did not receive the same offer it was noteworthy that the UK PC warranty company Direct Care almost immediately offered a PC, through their Online Direct ISP, to their members for £299 instead of the normal £450. It may well be that the growth business is now in the ISP market rather than the PC market. This does make good business growth sense. Users who receive a free or heavily discounted PC will (so the wisdom goes) then spend much more with the ISP providing the hardware. The costs to the ISP are not that high, the cost price of entry-level PCs having dropped rapidly over recent years.

Perhaps one of the reasons for AOL's success is the fact that it does not view itself as a technology company. It is a service company that allows people to access the fastest-growing communication and information medium – the Internet. By concentrating on service rather than technology AOL is able to relate most closely to its members, the vast majority of whom are technology users but not necessarily technically minded. It is very easy and inexpensive to access one's AOL email service from any Internet-connected terminal in the world, which means that members never need to be out of touch. This is a similar philosophy to that which has accounted for the success of Apple and Microsoft – they realize that things have to be made easy for the customer. They do the hard work; the customer reaps the benefit. AOL was amongst the first interactive online services providers to offer broadband to members. Figure 26 shows AOL's homepage.

Figure 26   AOL in the UK's homepage
Reproduced with permission of AOL.

The AOL product, like so many other products in the ICT sector, has been constantly updated. At the time of writing the mainstream product is AOL version 9.0. AOL 9.0 offers automatic scanning of email for **viruses**, spam protection and a range of AOL-specific channels that the member can access. Like all successful ISPs, AOL has proved easy to operate and that is what the average user requires. Email needs to be as easy to use as putting a stamp on a letter.

Stauffer, D. (2000), *Business the AOL Way* (Oxford: Capstone).

Java

Java is a programming language used in website development (see also Applet). Java Server Pages (pages with a .jsp **file extension**) technology enables web developers and designers to develop and easily maintain information-rich, dynamic web pages that leverage existing business systems. JSP technology is claimed to enable rapid development of web-based applications that are platform independent. JSP technology separates the user interface from content generation, enabling designers to change the overall page layout without altering the underlying dynamic content.

Javascript

Javascript was known as LiveScript until 1995 and is a programming language that allows a web designer the ability to easily insert code into a web page. Javascript is commonly placed into an **HTML** or a similar type of file and run directly from the web page to perform tasks such as printing the time and date, creating a calendar, or other tasks that are not possible through plain HTML.

Jaz

See **Iomega® Jaz**.

Journal

See **log**.

Joystick

A peripheral input device that looks similar to a game joystick that you would find on a gaming system. A computer joystick allows an individual to easily move an object in a game, such as navigating a plane in a flight simulator. In a more sophisticated form joysticks are used to operate the controls of some Airbus Industrie commercial jet aircraft, where they interface between the pilot and the aircraft's fly-by-wire computer systems, replacing the more traditional control column.

JPEG (Joint Photographic Experts Group)

JPEG is pronounced 'jay-peg'. JPEG is a **lossy compression** technique for colour images. Although it can reduce files sizes to about 5 per cent of their normal size, some detail is lost in the compression. A file that requires 470 KB as a JPEG file needs 8184 KB in **bitmap** format. JPEG files are often used for sending via email due to the fact that they are of reasonable **resolution** but do not require much memory and thus can be uploaded and downloaded fairly speedily.

JSP (Java Server Page)

Java Server Pages are an extension to the **Java servlet** technology.

JSPs have dynamic scripting capability that works in tandem with **HTML** code, separating the page logic from the static to help make the HTML more functional (for example, providing dynamic **database** queries).

A JSP is translated into Java servlet before being run, and it processes **HTTP** requests and generates responses like any servlet. However, JSP technology provides a more convenient way to code a servlet. JSPs are not restricted to any specific platform or server.

Keyboards

A keyboard still remains the main input mechanism for the vast majority of users notwithstanding developments in voice recognition software and touchscreens. Many Personal Digital Assistants (**PDAs**) have an option to use a keyboard instead of the touchscreen. It was thought that the growth in computers might lead to a change in keyboard design with A B C etc. replacing the traditional Q W E R T Y approach of the typewriter but this has not occurred. Even the most basic keyboard comes with special function keys (F1–F12) and a separate number pad. Many keyboards also have customized Internet keys that aid navigation. With the exception of laptops and notepads; where the keyboard is built in, it is usually connected to the computer by cable; Infra-red and wireless keyboards are now cheap and reliable. One of the limiting factors to the size of keyboards is that of the human finger – there is a lower limit below which it is impossible to hit a key without also depressing its neighbours.

Keyboards are available with the characters for different languages and it is possible to substitute a key physically and then allocate a different character to the stroke from that key. Thus a keyboard that only has one currency symbol can have that symbol assigned to £, $ or €. More advanced keyboards will have these as separate symbols.

Keywords

When referring to a search function a keyword is a word or group of words that helps the user locate a match for the search. Keywords are used by **search engines** for general Internet searches and also by specific websites such as AOL and amazon.com in order to locate specific items within the website. For example, an *amazon* search for a book can be made using the author, the title, the publisher, the ISBN (International Standard Book Number) or by keyword. Searching amazon.co.uk using the keywords 'Information', 'Communication' and 'Technology' sorted alphabetically returns over 1100 hits.

One of the problems with typing in a series of keywords is that superfluous results can often outnumber useful ones. Using an advanced search technique the user is able to filter the responses by a careful use of terms such as 'and', 'or' and 'not'. Advanced searches use **Boolean** expressions such as OR, AND, NOT. These can be used to create relationships among the keywords in the search query.

Figure 27 shows a list of expressions with their corresponding symbol (either can be used) and function.

Expression	Symbol	Action
AND	+	Finds documents containing all of the specified words or phrases. King + John finds documents with both the word John and the word King.
OR	I	Finds documents containing at least one of the specified words or phrases.
AND NOT	–	Attaching '–' in front of a word requires that the word not be found in any of the search results.

Figure 27   Boolean expressions used with keywords

K

Language

When referring to computer programming a language refers to the text, numbers and symbols written to create a software program.

When referring to a selection in a program a language commonly refers to what language the user of the computer speaks or prefers. For example, English may be an option. Word processors such as Word® offer a wide variety of languages. Word® offers 210 languages that can be checked for grammar and spelling, including 18 variants of English and no fewer than 20 versions of Spanish. Word® also offers basic translation, as do a number of **email** software packages.

Laptop

See **computer types – laptop.**

Large Scale Integration

A computer chip that contains between 100 and 5000 circuit elements. See also **Very Large Scale Integration (VLSI)** and **Ultra-Large Scale Integration**.

Licence agreements

The licence agreement is in effect the contract that defines the obligation a user must agree to before being able to use the software, such as not making copies other than those for backup, resale etc. When the user opens the software package this is an indication in law that he or she agrees to the licence agreement. New software may also require the user to agree to the licence before installing the program. In general the user will be required to click an 'Accept' or 'Disagree' button or check a box that says he or she accepts or disagrees with the agreement. Unless the box is checked the software installation will be paused.

Links

When referring to communications, a link is a connection between two devices. In data management or a file system a link refers to the capability of sharing or viewing shared information. On the **Internet** a link or **hyperlink** refers to a reference which points to another **web page**.

Linux

Linux was developed by Linus Torvalds (hence its name) with further work completed by a global network of developers. It is a freely available multi-tasking and multi-user operating system. From its inception Linux was placed under General Public Licence, meaning that the system can be distributed, used and expanded free of charge. This means that developers have access to all the required source codes and are thus able to integrate new functions easily or to find and eliminate programming bugs quickly. **Drivers** can be integrated very rapidly.

Liquid Crystal Display (LCD)

A type of display used in digital watches and clocks, display panels and many portable computers. LCD displays utilize two sheets of polarizing material with a liquid crystal solution between them. An electric current passed through the liquid causes the crystals to align so that light cannot pass through them. Each crystal, therefore, is like a shutter, either allowing light to pass through or blocking the light. Unlike traditional displays using light bulbs, LCDs do not give off heat or burn out.

Local Area Networks (LAN)

A communications network connecting a group of computers, printers and other devices located within a relatively limited area (for example, a single building). A LAN allows any connected device to interact with any other on the network. LANs (and their larger 'sibling' **WANs – Wide Area Networks**) have become powerful organizational tools in that they allow users to share information and devices.

The simplest type of LAN is that of a series of computers linked to and sharing a single device, for example a printer. A **server** attached to the printer allocates printing jobs and priorities. The extension of this is to link all of the computers across a **network**. The example shown in Figure 28 has the network linked by a **serial bus**.

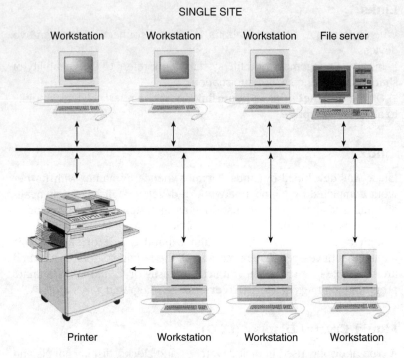

Figure 28 A simple Local Area Network (LAN)

In designing a LAN a number of important criteria need to be borne in mind:

- How easy will it be to extend the network for new users and devices? Wiring via a serial bus can be useful as this allows new workstation connections etc. to be added relatively simply without the need to rewire the whole system.
- Will upgrading be simple, especially when it needs to be done across the network? This implies the need to consider whether software is to be held centrally and accessed by workstations or held at the workstation (or indeed a combination of both).
- How will the LAN be connected to external networks such as a Wide Area Network (WAN)?
- Even the simplest LAN will need a **file server** and a **print server**. As the network grows, more of these need to be in place plus a **communication server** to facilitate **Internet** and **WAN** connections.

L

- A dedicated **Network Operating System** will also need to be employed.

Typically Local Area Networks are cabled using ethernet cabling (usually around 10 mm in thickness). Thick ethernet cabling with a copper core can support up to 100 workstations or devices whilst thin ethernet cabling that has a stranded cable core) supports up to 30. More sophisticated LAN installations may use **fibre optics** to transmit **data**.

Mikalsen, A. and Borgsen, P. (2002), *Local Area Network Management, Design and Security: A Practical Approach* (Chichester: Wiley).

Steinke, S. (ed.) (1996), *LAN Tutorial: A Complete Introduction to Local Area Networks (LAN Networking Library)* (London: CMP – Miller Freeman).

Log

A log or **journal** is a detailed list of a system's or application's activities (see Figure 29). A log can be useful for keeping track of computer use and emergency recovery of data. Each software program that is capable of creating a log has different methods of starting or stopping the log creation.

Logical operator

One of the logical functions such as AND, OR, NOT etc. used on variables.

Lossy compression

Refers to data compression techniques in which some amount of data is lost. Lossy compression technologies attempt to eliminate redundant or unnecessary information. Graphic and video compression technologies, such as JPEG and MPEG, use a lossy technique.

L

Loyalty cards

The 1990s saw a proliferation of loyalty schemes, in part due to the opportunities presented by the introduction of new information and communication technology systems. Loyalty schemes have, however, been around for some considerable time. Since the earliest days of commercial activity, discounts have been offered to repeat customers to encourage them to come back to the same supplier. What new technology has allowed is for loyalty schemes to become highly sophisticated.

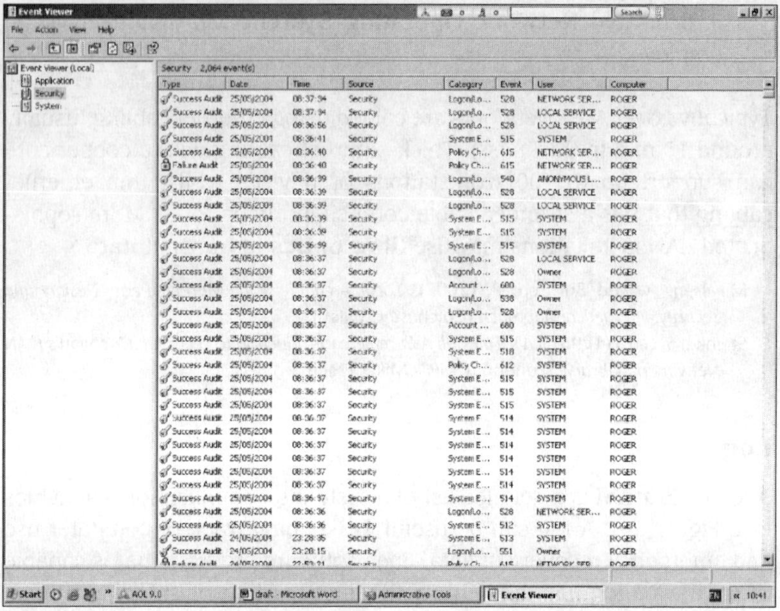

Figure 29 Part of a PC's security log

The most important attribute of a successful scheme is that the customer perceives added value. If they do not, then the scheme is doomed. To add value it must offer benefits that the customer wants as opposed to those that the organization may wish to give. In addition a loyalty scheme must also:

- be mutually beneficial;
- reward increased spending;
- be a vehicle for enhanced communication;
- be cost effective;
- be able to operate across an organization's sites in the case of a multi-site organization.

In the current climate it is also useful if a loyalty scheme can operate across organizations by rewarding spending at the premises of a variety of participating organizations.

Whilst the logistics of operating loyalty schemes may be complex, they are eased by the ability of computers to communicate very effectively. The use of customer data contained within loyalty cards has enabled organizations to gain extra benefit from loyalty schemes as they can track customers' spending patterns and gain valuable general and highly personal information.

The Tesco Clubcard has been one of the most successful loyalty and promotional schemes since its introduction in 1995. At that time UK supermarkets were undergoing a major expansion especially in the form of 'edge of town' sites offering increased facilities. Whilst Sunday trading had been the norm in Scotland for many years, changes in the law in England in the 1990s allowed the supermarkets to offer a seven-day-per-week service. Many sites now offer a seven-day, 24-hour operation. The provision of ample parking spaces, café facilities, cash dispensers, florists and an increasing product range was allowing a successful supermarket operation to become a 'one-stop shop' for customers. The competition for suitable sites that provided both the space needed for customer vehicles and proximity to major roads and motorways was intense and the supermarkets were keen not only to acquire new customers but to retain those customers in order to boost their market share. The Tesco Clubcard scheme recorded the monetary value of a customer's purchases at the till point and then sent the customer a series of 'money off' vouchers according to the spend made. The scheme was very successful and by June 1996 there were over eight million members.

It has been claimed that the Clubcard scheme assisted Tesco in boosting its turnover by 25 per cent and profits by 15 per cent in its first year of operation despite the fact that over £40 million had been given back to customers as a result of Clubcard discounts.

The Clubcard scheme in its original form provided for discounts on spending at Tesco but by 1999 members could receive discounts at theme parks, on holidays, air tickets, entertainments, rail travel, ferry crossings and a host of other products and services. To this extent Clubcard has moved nearer to the Airmiles concept.

It is not surprising that Tesco's competitors have followed suit. Loyalty schemes in the UK have flourished, mirroring the US experience, and nearly every purse and wallet contains a series of such cards issued by a variety of organizations.

The advantage to the retailer is in the relatively inexpensive access gained to valuable market information. A profile of a regular customer can be compiled if required, though naturally such data is covered by the data protection legislation. Knowing details of the customer can increase the overall market knowledge that an organization has about its customer base and this can provide it with a competitive advantage.

Loyalty cards are just one way in which organizations are using ICT to improve their understanding of the markets within which they operate. The ability of **card readers** to acquire data about the customer very quickly and with no fuss, coupled to the ability of the computer systems to analyse the buying patterns, is what makes loyalty cards so powerful – another example of **synergy**.

Cartwright, R. (2000), *Mastering Customer Relations* (Basingstoke: Palgrave Macmillan).

L

Machine code

Machine code (or machine language as it is also known) is the only language a computer is actually capable of understanding. Machine code or machine language is a collection of **binary** digits or bits that the computer reads and interprets.

Machine language

See **machine code.**

Macro

A macro is a series of instructions designed to simplify repetitive tasks within a program such as Microsoft Word®, Excel or Access. Macros execute when a user opens the associated file or when instructed to do so by the programming.

Macromedia Flash

See **Flash.**

Mail merge

The capability of **word processor**, **database** and some email programs that takes a standard form and formats it with unique fields such as email address, name, address, phone number, or other personal information to make the message look unique despite the fact it is just a standard letter with personalized details. This ability has been used to produce books for children that include the child's name at appropriate places. Mail merge is an inexpensive means of appearing to deliver a more personalized service. Great care must be taken in setting out the form if anomalies are not to occur, such as referring to somebody as Mr Doctor Jones (in German Herr Doktor is perfectly acceptable).

Mailing list

Discussion groups over the Internet that link a number of people with common interests together via email.

A mailing list may also be used to describe a list of email addresses. This is often referred to as an address book.

See also **address book.**

Majordormo

A free mailing-list server that runs using **UNIX**. When email is addressed to a Majordomo mailing list it is automatically broadcast to everyone on the list. The result is similar to a newsgroup or forum except that the messages are transmitted as email and are therefore available only to individuals on the list.

Malware

See **adware.**

Management Information Systems (MIS)

Modern management is able to benefit from the advances in computer technology that make large amounts of information and data easier to analyse. A Management Information System (MIS) can be defined as the people, equipment and processes required to gather, sort, analyse, evaluate and distribute both timely and accurate management information to the key decision makers. Information technology can aid the whole of this process using both data processing and email.

A Management Information System is used to hold financial, human resource, operational, customer etc. information. Its power is that it is an integrated system that allows connections to be made between various organizational functions. MIS also serves to break down departmental barriers as the information (unless restricted for confidentiality reasons) should be available to all managers. This places an emphasis on the need to train managers in understanding the roles of others. There is little point in giving a production manager access to the finance information in the MIS if he or she has received no training in understanding the finance function. Advances in Information and Communication Technology may make disseminating information easier but it does not absolve organizations from the need to ensure that the information can be understood and acted upon.

Manuals – book format

In the early days of computer growth, new systems came with huge manuals, the majority of which remained unread on shelves. These manuals contained huge amounts of superfluous material that may have been useful to an Information Technology (IT) specialist but was of little use to the average user who was more interested in applications. These paper-based manuals have largely been replaced by on-screen **help**, **on-line help** and **PDF** manuals. What have also proved useful are publications such as the 'Dummies' or 'Complete Idiot's Guide' series that provide a useful guide to software applications.

ICT specialists still require more complex manuals and these are readily available from most bookshops but the majority of computers for home and small business use now come with very little paper-based supporting documentation.

Gookin, D. (2003), *Microsoft Office – WORD 2003 for Dummies* (Hoboken, NJ: Wiley).

Manuals – electronic

As a replacement for the bulky electronic manuals, those requiring more detailed information than that available as on-screen or on-line **help** can often download a manual written in Portable Document Format (**PDF**) format. This allows the user to print out only the items of particular interest.

Mapped drives

Network drives assigned local drive letters and locally accessible. For example, the directory path \BOOKS\JICT\ might be mapped as drive F (a CDR drive): on a computer.

Memory

In general terms memory is the fast **semiconductor** storage (Random Access Memory – **RAM**) directly connected to the processor, which depends on electrical power for activation. Once the power is turned off the data in the RAM is lost. Memory is often differentiated from computer storage (for example, hard disks, floppy disks and CD-ROM disks) as these do not depend on permanent electricity connections and are therefore a more permanent means for holding data. Memory and storage are measured in **bytes** (usually kilo, mega or giga bytes – see Introduction).

M

Menus

A menu is a list of commands and/or choices offered to the user in a list. Menus are commonly used in a **GUI** environment and allow a user to quickly access the various options the software program is capable of performing. File menus are commonly accessed using the computer's mouse or trackerball. Some menu commands can be accessed direct from the keyboard using shortcuts. (See Figure 30 for an example.)

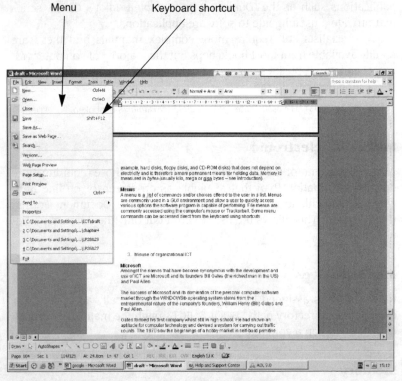

Figure 30   A menu brought up over a page in Word®

MICR (Magnetic Ink Character Recognition)

MICR is a type of font capable of recognition using magnetically charged ink. Computers equipped with the right hardware and software can print and/or read the characters printed in such ink.

MICR font is commonly used to print cheques and deposit slips for banks where there is a need to read the account numbers into the computer. There are various types of MICR fonts for different alphabets depending on the country in question. Whilst a fairly simple technology, MICR has proved to be very useful in transferring simple data from paper to computer systems.

Microsoft

Amongst the names that have become synonymous with the development and use of ICT are Microsoft and its founders Bill Gates (the richest man in the USA) and Paul Allen. The success of Microsoft and its domination of the personal computer software market through the Windows® operating system stems from the entrepreneurial nature of the company's founders.

Gates formed his first company while still in high school. He had shown an aptitude for computer technology and devised a system for carrying out traffic counts. The year 1970 saw the beginnings of a hobby market in self-build primitive computers. The introduction of kits for the Altair 880 system in 1975 provided Gates and Allen with the opportunity to build software to use on the machine. Interestingly, software was the neglected area of development. At that time the 'intellectual' stimulation of building a machine that would work seemed to be the main focus of hobbyists. It was very astute and highly entrepreneurial of Gates and Allen to realize that their futures lay not in designing and supplying hardware but in providing the software for such machines.

Gates's great contribution may well be remembered not so much in the names of his products but in his realization that the developing IT (information technology) sector would eventually require standardization. In the beginning each machine used its own, sometimes unique, operating system. Gates foresaw that compatibility would be the route to success. Gates made deals with **OEMs (Original Equipment Manufacturers)** that put his software onto their machines (for more information see the entry for **OEM**).

It was but a short step from having applications available for a new computer system at its launch to having it already pre-installed, making the whole package ready to run from the box – a considerable boon to the growing number of users who had no interest in computers as technology but who needed the applications for their work and pleasure. They did not want to go through a process of installing software; they wanted the whole package ready to run.

The development of Windows® as an operating environment (originally by Apple but later becoming a name synonymous with Microsoft) allowed for multifunctionality and multi-tasking to be offered to even the most inexperienced user. Packages such as Microsoft Office, containing as they do a word processor (Word®) and a spreadsheet (Excel®) etc., provide for a complete set of applications using similar commands and icons all in a mouse-driven, Windows® environment.

The very earliest machines were devoid of the hard disks and even monitors that are the norm today. In order to start up the hardware it had to be booted (derived from 'pulling it up by the bootstraps'), adding an operating system to the small amount of resident instructions.

As an internal hard disk became the norm it was necessary to develop what we now know as DOS (Disk Operating System) software to manage the computer system (see the section on **operating systems**). Microsoft's growth is in part because of the development of MS (Microsoft) DOS as this standardized operating system has become the platform upon which Windows® can be placed and the myriad of Microsoft and other Windows® compatible applications run. Microsoft has made compatibility its stock in trade, compatibility that is actually on its own terms as Microsoft has been setting the compatibility standards, – in effect, writing the rules – and nothing is as fundamental in the computer business as the operating system.

In 1964, as a result of an NSF (National Science Foundation) grant, John Chimney and Thomas Kurt at Dartmouth College ran the first example of a new programming language called BASIC (Beginners All-purpose Symbolic Instruction Code). The important thing about BASIC was that it began the process of demystifying programming. It was an object lesson in simplicity. When the user wanted the computer to do something it was just a matter of a few simple lines of code:

```
10   New
20   PRINT 5 + 3
```
If RUN was then typed the legend:
```
8
```
appeared on the screen.

In the 1970s this was wonderful and cutting edge!

One of the problems was that there were many forms of BASIC and they all used slightly different syntax etc. In essence they were dialects and programmers needed to learn a number of variations. By developing MS (Microsoft) BASIC, the company was able to develop a single basic type. The provision of MS BASIC + MS DOS by OEMs (see earlier) allowed the computer manufacturers to offer a hardware/software package to customers that did not require any relearning of commands and operating protocols.

Apple computers were the first to offer an operating environment that used a mouse and icons to point and click rather than keyboard inputs. Indeed one idea was to remove the keyboard completely, as some of the small hand-held organizers and computers have done. This has become known as Windows® and has its own section later in this text.

It is hardly surprising that so many of the world's computers come pre-loaded with Microsoft products, and not in the least sinister. Microsoft took an entrepreneurial decision to work with OEMs and provide applications for different computers. That was clearly a sensible commercial decision. Unfortunately the world has become so dependent on computer technologies that any monopoly looks dangerous, hence the recent legal actions against Microsoft by the US government and the European Union.

Like Coca-Cola, Boeing and Shell, the word Microsoft is a global term, no matter where one is there will probably be a computer running Windows®. Microsoft has not been beyond criticism. OEMs were very good at finding software bugs as they tested their machines before putting them out into the market. Once Microsoft began to supply retailers who dealt directly with the public such bugs were not as easily tolerated. It must be stressed, however, that Microsoft appears to have worked hard at minimizing the effects of such bugs and has rectified any problems quickly. Computers do still crash because of the software but such occurrences seem to be becoming rarer.

Dearlove, D. (2001), *Doing Business the Bill Gates Way* (Oxford: Capstone).
Manes, S. and Andrews, P. (1994), *Gates* (New York: Simon & Schuster).

Microchip

The heart of the ICT revolution – a microchip – is a very small silicon-based **integrated circuit** or **integrated chip**. First developed in 1958 by Jack Kilby and Robert Noyce, a microchip is a package containing many circuits, pathways, semiconductors and other electronic components all working together to perform a particular function or a series of functions. Such integrated circuits are the building blocks of computer hardware.

MIDI (Musical Instrument Digital Interface)

MIDI is a global standard for **digitally** representing and transmitting sounds allowing electronic devices such as keyboards and computer sound cards to understand. The MIDI sound is played back through the hardware device or computer either through a synthesized audio sound or a waveform stored on the hardware device or computer. The quality of how MIDI sounds when played back by the hardware device or computer depends upon that particular device's capability.

Misuse of organizational ICT

Organizations spend a great deal of money on their ICT systems. In addition to the initial costs, the system also needs to be maintained, upgraded and protected from attack by **viruses**, **trojans**, **worms** and **hacking**.

Not surprisingly, the vast majority of organizations have implemented policies and procedures governing the use and misuse of ICT. ICT in its various guises has always been open to misuse. Even simple telephone technology can be misused by employees making and receiving personal calls on their employer's telephones. Whilst few employers object to the odd personal call made with permission, the employee who uses a work telephone as though it were his or her personal domestic one is actually committing fraud (just as using the employer's postage stamps for personal mail is also fraudulent).

Email and access to the Internet has provided extra opportunities for misuse. At its worst such misuse can involve the giving away of the organization's data and proprietary information. Even using email for personal use can be detrimental to the organization's efficient operation, in that it can clog up the system especially if the individual receives quantities of **spam**. There is also the danger that the individual will upset somebody in a personal email and that person may respond by a complaint against the organization (in the UK organizations can in certain circumstances have a vicarious liability if employees use the organization's equipment for their personal use) or even an attack on the organization's **ICT** systems.

Internet access is often carefully controlled with personal use being prohibited. There have been a number of high-profile cases of dismissal of employees who have used organizational ICT systems to access (and in some cases download from) inappropriate and sometimes illegal sites, especially those with pornographic content.

Mobile computers

See under **laptops**, **notebooks** and **PDAs**.

Modelling

See **applications/software – modelling**.

Modem (modulator/demodulator)

A device that allows computer information to be transmitted and received over a telephone line. The transmitting modem translates digital computer data into **analogue** signals that can be carried over a phone line. The receiving modem translates the analogue signals back to **digital** form. Most PCs come fitted with a 56 K modem and those wishing to use ADSL/broadband need to fit a faster modem. The speed is the maximum that the modem can cope with. In practice any problems with the telephone line are likely to decrease the figure.

Modem compression

A technique used to reduce the number of characters transmitted without losing data content. The transmitting modem compresses the data and the receiving computer or modem decompresses the data back to its original state.

Modulation standards

Protocols that determine how modems convert digital data into analogue signals that can be transmitted over telephone lines.

Initially the Bell Company created modulation standards used in the United States and the International telephone Union (ITU) created international recommendations. The ITU-T (formerly called the CCITT) now makes recommendations generally adopted by modem manufacturers across the globe. Standardization is obviously necessary given the growth in networks.

Monitors

The most common means of displaying computer output is via a screen or monitor. In the early days of computer use results were printed on sheets of paper or paper ribbons. Today, although final output may be by printer, the work carried out on the computer is usually 'monitored' via a screen.

Early monitors used the standard television technology of cathode ray tubes, which were quite bulky and could generate considerable quantities of heat. The recent trend, pioneered in **laptop** and **notebook** computers, has been for a flat **Thin Film Transistor (TFT)** screen to be employed. This does not generate heat, does not have the flickering that can fatigue the eye and has a smaller **footprint** and clearer display. In the same way that computers first derived their monitors from televisions, so televisions are now being produced with flat TFT screens. **Touchscreen** technology, as used in many **Personal Digital Assistants (PDAs)**, allows the monitor to become an input as well as an output device.

Motherboard

Also referred to as the mainboard, mobo or system board. The motherboard is a printed circuit that is the foundation of a computer and allows the **CPU**, **RAM** and other computer components to function with each other.

Mouse

Next to a keyboard a mouse is the most common input device for computers. A mouse (and the closely related **trackerball**) allows an individual to control a mouse pointer in a Graphical User Interface (**GUI**). A mouse gives the user the ability to perform various functions such as opening a program or file and does not require the user to memorize a series of commands – the mouse pointer can simply be used to click on the **menu**.

A mouse (originally named after its shape and 'tail' – wireless versions have lost this feature) may be connected via cable, infra-red or wireless. For a PC a mouse has right and left buttons for clicking on menus etc. and often contains a scroll wheel feature that allows the user fast navigation up and down a page on the screen.

MPEG (Motion Picture Experts Group)

Widely used video **codec** used by most computers to display a video. MPEG compression is capable of being handled through the software and/or hardware. The high quality of an MPEG is achieved by discarding any image data that will not be easily detected by the human eye. MPEG files have the file extension .mpg/.mpeg.

MP3

MP3 is a file and compression method utilizing MPEG compression to reduce the size of a file. MP3 files are commonly used to store music and require very little hard disk space compared to other types of files. Because of the file size it is possible for a user to store vast quantities of songs or pieces of music on a computer. In addition to being able to store MP3 files, users can also because of the size share MP3 files with other Internet users. This has resulted in many songs and CDs being downloaded from various file-sharing services without the purchase of the original CDs. This has led to legal arguments over MP3 use.

It is possible to purchase portable dedicated MP3 players, which allow the user to take music with him or her without the need to carry a large number of CDs.

MSN® (Microsoft Network)

Microsoft's own **Internet Service Provider (ISP)** offering comparable services to other subscription ISPs.

Multimedia

Multimedia is a display that is a combination of audio, video, animation and graphics. Multimedia has found a ready function in both the worlds of education and entertainment, where there can be a seamless transition and synergy between the various types of media.

Multiplexer

A circuit or other type of device that allows several devices to send data over a single communication line. The communication line is high speed and is able to handle packets of data from a number of low-speed devices.

One commonly found application of multiplex technology, indeed the application that brought it into a more public domain, is that of commercial aircraft entertainment systems. When Boeing was developing the 747 'Jumbo Jet' in the 1960s, the aircraft represented a huge advance in the numbers of passengers to be carried – up to 500 in some configurations. This meant that a huge number of wires needed to be taken to each seat for the growing number of entertainment options travellers required. Traditional wiring would be too heavy; Boeing needed to conserve as much weight as possible. If one channel could carry packets of data from several devices this would save considerable wiring and the attendant weight associated with the wires. It took some time to work out the problems associated with multiplex but today the technology allows travellers to have a huge range of features at their seat and on a personal screen in front of them.

M

Irving, C. (1993), *Wide Body: The Making of the Boeing 747* (London: Hodder & Stoughton).

Multipoint

Channel or other type of communication device where many devices share a single communication line. This ability removes the need for separate channels for each device and is very important in **networks**.

Multiprocessing system

Such a system provides a computer with the ability to utilize two or more processors for computer operations. With multiple processors the computer performance can be significantly increased. On standard home computers not all standard applications will utilize two or more processors in a computer, therefore multiple processors may not be fully utilized and the user may not notice a speed increase.

Multi-tasking

In management terms multi-tasking is the allocation of a number of roles to an individual who may, therefore need to become multi-skilled. As ICT has become so important and a part of everyday work and domestic life so individuals need to accept ICT roles in addition to their normal functional role. ICT skills in terms of using applications are now an everyday part of work life.

   In the early days of ICT much of the so-called 'computing', including mundane tasks such as **word processing**, was carried out by specialist tasks. ICT developments allow these tasks to be carried out by anybody in the organization using their desktop computer. All staff therefore need ICT skills. Multitasking can also refer to the ability of a computer to run a number of applications at the same time. This can give the impression of simultaneous processing, which it is not – it is only the speed with which each application is accessed that gives the impression that everything is being done at the same time.

Network

The development of the telephone in the early part of the twentieth century placed exchange systems between users so that telephone A could communicate with all other telephones in the same network via the exchange (see Figure 31).

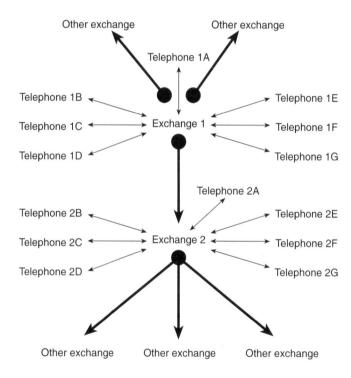

Figure 31 A telephone network

The next development was to link the exchanges of different telephone networks, firstly within one country and then internationally by using, firstly, wires and later radio transmission via satellites and **fibre optics**. By the latter years of the twentieth century it was possible to telephone from almost any part of the world to anywhere else in the world without operator intervention because exchanges had become automatic (known in the UK as Subscriber Trunk Dialling – STD). Considerable efforts had been made from the middle of the nineteenth century to put a global communication's infrastructure into place. This is an important point as it means that the infrastructure to support the Internet was already in place prior to the development of the electronic computer. Computers handle information using digital technology – telephone lines, fibre optics and radio signals are excellent mediums for the transmission of digital impulses.

An ICT network is a group of computers and other devices, for example **printers** and **scanners**, connected by a communications link (cable, fibre optics or wireless), enabling all the devices to interact with each other. Networks can be small or large, permanently connected through wires or cables, or temporarily connected through phone lines or wireless transmissions. The largest network is the Internet, which is a worldwide group of networks. It is networks that have made ICT as important as it is today.

One of the key concepts that underlies the importance of networks is that of connectivity. We can look at connectivity in a simple way using unidirectional straight lines (bi-directional lines double the number of possibilities).

2 dots (or devices) can be linked by a straight line in only one way:

Using 3 dots produces 3 links:

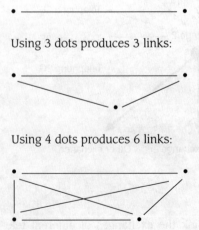

Using 4 dots produces 6 links:

The actual series or progression is as shown below:

Points	2	3	4	5	6	7	8	9	10
Links	1	3	6	10	15	21	28	36	45

The more computers a single computer is linked to, the greater is the amount of information it can access. The user does not need to rely solely on information stored within his or her computer but is able to access information stored on all the linked computers. When one considers the number of computers linked to the Internet (at least 150,000,000), the number of linkages is an astronomic sum!

Networks are connected in three basic types – bus, star and ring – each with its own advantages and disadvantages.

The advantages of a bus network (see Figure 32) are that it is easy to wire as new computers and devices can be wired into the bus. A building can thus have a cable run installed as it is built and the devices are just attached via connectors to the cable. However, if the main cable fails then all the machines that lie beyond the break from the server will be affected. The more computers and devices that are added, the slower the network will be. There is a working limit, depending on the equipment used, when using co-axial cable and also a maximum recommended distance between the connections on the network if wire rather than fibre-optic connections are used.

A star network (see Figure 33) requires dedicated connections between each computer and the server, which makes it more expensive to install and more complex to operate. However, a failure in one cable leaves all the others operable.

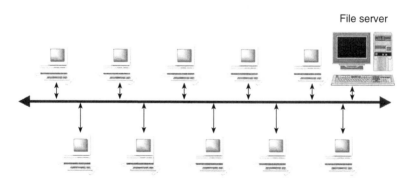

Figure 32 A bus network

N

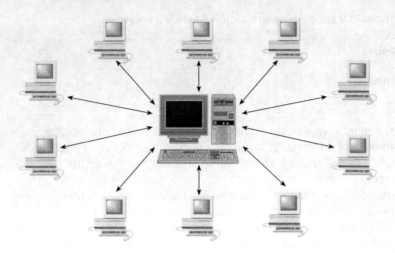

Figure 33 A star network

A ring network (see Figure 34) is unidirectional, which makes it fast, and it is not too difficult to put a machine in place between existing ones. It shares the problem, however, like the bus network, that a break in the cable affects the whole system.

Those planning networks need to balance the risk of a cable failure or break with the need for speed and expansion of the network when deciding which format to adopt.

Computers within a network usually have an extra **drive** – a network drive. Data can be stored on the computer's drive, in which case it is only available for access via that machine or on the network drive at the **server** and is then available across the network.

Freed, L. and Defler, F. (2002), *How Networks Work* (London: Que).

Network administrator

Networks do not manage themselves. It is usual for organizations to appoint a network or systems manager to be responsible for planning, configuring and managing the day-to-day operation of the network. The post of network manager is a demanding one as the person appointed needs not only technical ability but a knowledge of the workings of the organization and the needs of the various departments and individuals within it. The network manager needs to ensure that the network serves the working of the organization and not the other way around.

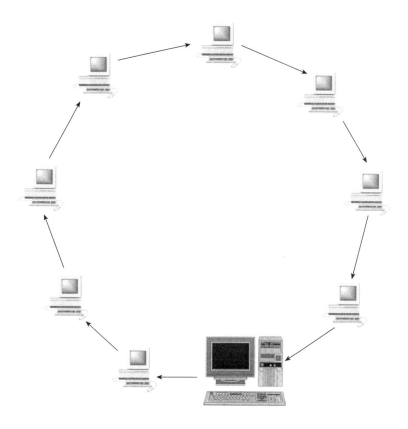

Figure 34 A ring network

Network cards

If a computer is to be used in a network it needs to have a network card fitted onto or linked to the **motherboard**. The network card enables data to pass between the computer and the network cables. To ensure that data is delivered correctly to the computer, each network card has its own unique address.

N

Network protocol

The language a computer uses to communicate over a network. For a computer to communicate with another computer, they must both use the same **protocol** or use software that allows protocols to interface with each other.

Newsgroups

An electronic forum where readers post articles and follow-up messages on a specified topic. An Internet newsgroup allows people from around the globe to discuss common interests. Newsgroups may be public, available to subscribers (such as those run by AOL) or by invitation only, in which case they will be protected by **passwords** etc.

Other names that are used include on-line discussion groups, web forums and message boards. On a message board messages are 'threaded' together to aid the subscriber in following a train of thought. Newsgroups groups differ from chat rooms in that the messages travel back and forth a bit slower and they are usually archived for a fairly long period of time. Newsgroups are good places to gather information on a topic.

The specific term 'newsgroup' was initially associated with Usenet – a network that predates the World Wide Web. There are thousands of discussion groups in this system – some of which are the most active in the world. In fact, Usenet predates the Web by about 20 years and exists outside of the **HTML** universe. That means that a user requires a separate piece of software for participation in Usenet groups.

A useful site on which to look for newsgroups is the Tile Net website. Mailing lists can be searched for by using the Liszt directory website. The following are some of the subject areas that can be accessed:

comp	computer-related subjects
news	information about newsgroups themselves
rec	recreational subjects – hobbies, sports etc.
sci	science
soc	social issues
talk	politics, religion etc.
misc	miscellaneous subjects
alt	alternative subjects
biz	business subjects
courts	legal issues
de	German
fj	Japan

N

Whilst many newsgroups are interactive there are also mailing lists that are read only. Subscribers to these groups receive newsletters via email but are not able to post messages.

Newsgroups have both advantages and disadvantages. They are useful in that they link a user to those of like mind. Like all text-based communications they cannot provide body language or intonation clues within the communication process and thus it may be difficult to ascertain precisely what a contributor really thinks.

It is relatively easy to remain anonymous within a newsgroup but this can lead to behaviour that would be unacceptable in a face-to-face situation or where the offender's name was known. Newsgroups have their own etiquette. They are often moderated, i.e. there is a webmaster who will remove any posts that are offensive. A person making such posts may be barred from the newsgroup altogether. As the 'discussions' in a newsgroup occur in cyberspace there might be those who believe that the usual rules of behaviour do not apply. They do. Users of newsgroups should never:

- post messages that are in any way threatening to anybody;
- use obscene language in a post;
- attempt to sell items to other subscribers unless the newsgroup is one that allows selling;
- post messages that are not relevant to the newsgroup.

Those who fail to behave properly may well find their posts being removed and themselves excluded from the newsgroup altogether. Making threats etc. can lead to criminal investigation.

Noise

In ICT terms noise is anything that reduces the effectiveness of the transmission of an electronic communication. An electronic or even physical problem on a telephone line can reduce the transmission speed of a modem from, say, 56 Kps to 48 (or lower) Kps. This constitutes noise. New cabling technologies especially the use of **fibre optics**, remove noise completely as it is an electrical phenomenon. These technologies thus both speed up data transmission and reduce the risk of data being corrupted in transit.

N

Oo

OCR (Optical Character Recognition)

OCR software is used by scanners to recognize characters as opposed to shape. Switching to OCR mode instructs the computer that the material being dealt with is text rather than graphics. The current software is good but careful editing is still required as not every font variant will be recognized. Optical Character Recognition has aided users as they are able to scan in text from external paper-based sources without the need to type it in to the computer first, a process that can be very laborious especially if there is a considerable amount of text.

OEM (Original Equipment Manufacturer)

Many of the early computer enterprises were concerned with the development of small machines suitable for desktop use, what has become known as the PC (Personal Computer) market – a term originally applied to the products of IBM (International Business Machines), a company that entered the domestic/small business market quite late having previously concentrated on mainframe hardware. Many of the names now belong to history but PET, Sirius, Apricot etc. were the first generation of office computers and needed applications to run on them. From early on users required word processing and spreadsheets, WordStar and SuperCalc being two of the earliest examples of applications written for different machines but overlaid on the operating system so that the same commands would operate them once the machine was booted. There was also a growing games market – primitive as the early offerings were, users realized the 'fun' and entertainment potential of computers.

Although there might have been a temptation to go into hardware manufacture, Bill Gates of Microsoft took the view that the future of the company lay in providing applications etc. for a range of hardware and that Microsoft should enter into partnership agreements with OEMs (Original Equipment Manufacturers). Microsoft would provide the Disk Operating System and applications for a manufacturer's machines and whilst each version might be slightly different due to the design of the hardware, the user would not notice this. The concept of a 'one size fits all' approach to software is what has made Microsoft the force in the world that it is today. No matter who made the hardware, Microsoft, by forming an early partnership with that OEM, would have software available by the time the equipment reached the market.

The next step, again led by Microsoft, went from having applications available for a new computer system at its launch to having them pre-installed, making the whole package ready to run from the box – a considerable boon to the growing number of users who had no interest in computers as technology but who needed the applications for their work and pleasure. Packaging meant that they need not go through a process of installing software as all they were likely to require would be ready to run.

The development of Windows® as an operating environment (originally by Apple but later becoming a name synonymous with Microsoft) allowed for multifunctionality and multitasking to be offered to even the most inexperienced user. Packages such as Microsoft Office® containing as they do a word processor (Word®) and a spreadsheet (Excel®) etc., provide for a complete set of applications using similar commands and icons all in a mouse-driven, Windows® environment. Microsoft is not alone in offering such packages although it is certainly the global market leader.

Off-line

Term used to describe when a connection is broken or disconnected. When a device is off-line it is unable to send or receive information through that device. A printer can only print when it is on-line, i.e. switched on and connected to a computer. In terms of the Internet, off-line has a different meaning, as described under **off-line web pages**.

Web content can also be cached and stored off-line (see off-line web pages).

Off-line web pages

O

Off-line viewing of web pages involves the downloading of web pages to the computer's cache on the hard disk and then viewing with the computer disconnected from the Internet. As the pages are then accessed from the hard disk the speed of loading and display is far greater.

The advantage of off-line viewing are:

- no ISP charges are incurred;
- no telephone charges are incurred;

- the telephone line remains available for other use;
- there is faster loading and display of pages;
- the user can read the page at his or her own speed.

The disadvantages of off-line viewing are:

- unavailability of links;
- the page may not be the latest version.

Provided a page has been saved onto the computer's hard disk it is possible to use a feature known as Synchronise whilst connected to the Internet. The browser will then ensure that the most up-to-date version of the page is available off-line.

On-line

The term used to describe when a connection is made between one device and another. When a device is on-line it is able to send and/or receive information. An Internet user is on-line when he or she has an open connection to the Internet.

On-line banking

An individual's relationship with their bank used to be a very personal one, with the manger knowing the vast majority of the branch's customers by name. In the UK for many years after the Second World War, banks were open six days per week, offering a Saturday morning service, although they tended to open later and shut earlier than the vast majority of retailers and other businesses.

When the banks decided to stop Saturday opening, business was lost to the building societies that were open on Saturdays, a time when many people wished to withdraw cash for shopping. The introduction of **ATMs** (cash machines) allowed customers to withdraw cash at any time and now virtually every bank and building society offers this facility. However, there are other transactions people need to make with their banks and for those at work or in remote locations or who have disabilities, contact with the bank during normal business hours can be difficult.

One method the banks and building societies have used to solve this problem is the introduction of call centres using telephone technology, where information and certain transactions can be undertaken. Many such centres have extended access hours and indeed the trend is towards a 24-hour service. This provides the customer with greater time to contact their bank but at a further distance and with a less personal service. Many of these call centres are located in locations far remote from both the bank and its customers. In recent years many UK banks have set up call centres in India due to the economic advantages they perceive through lower costs.

The other method that is growing rapidly is the development of on-line banking linking the customer's personal computer with the bank. The first UK bank to introduce such a service was the Bank of Scotland, which offered its HOBS (Home and Office Banking Service) to selected customers from 1993. This system required a special modem, though whilst quite revolutionary for the time, would seem very slow today. Working through the DOS system, HOBS basically allowed customers to check their balances, a facility not available on the ATMs of the time, but commonplace today.

Modern on-line banking allows, in most cases, for customers not only to check their balance but to print out statements, pay bills, transfer monies between accounts and to download data with other types of software, e.g. accounts packages. Customers can apply for an overdraft or loan on-line.

The advantages to the banks are self-evident. Branches cost money both in terms of staff and premises; on-line banking costs far less. The customer is able to conduct the vast majority of day-to-day transactions at his or her convenience. The personal touch is, of course, lost and it remains problematic as to whether the branch network will completely disappear. The trend throughout the 1990s has been for mergers between banks; for building societies to convert to banks; and for branch networks to be cut. Provided that there is a human being available for those transactions that are not standard but require discussion and negotiation, then the future of on-line banking seems set to grow.

The challenge for the banks and building societies is to find a method for making the customer feel personally valued. Many of the banks and building societies, recognizing this need, have introduced the concept of a 'personal banker' whom the customer can contact in the event of problems. Most transactions can be carried out quickly and conveniently on-line or on the telephone to any member of the bank's staff but the 'personal banker' is available to discuss and rectify any problems.

A key issue in Internet banking is that of security. Many banks have reported that there have been attempts to obtain personal details from customers, with a view to possible fraud. Multilayered **PIN numbers** and **passwords** together with **HTTPS** protection is provided to ensure security and confidence in the system.

Winder. D. (1999),'On Line Banking', in *PC Pro*, issue 57 (July 1999), pp. 206–18.

On-line gambling

It has not taken the gambling industry long to discover that the Internet and a credit card allow gamblers 24-hour global access to their products. Many different types of gambling are now available on-line.

On-line help

A **help** function that is available on-line. Such help allows the user to ask questions of technical experts and chat to other users (see Figure 35). The help provider can ensure that the latest information is always available and that any **patches** are available for downloading.

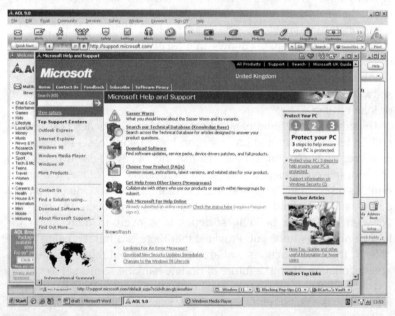

Figure 35 An on-line help and support page
Screenshot reprinted by permission from Microsoft Corporation.

On-line news and information

Many **Internet Service Providers (ISPs)**, **search engines**, newspapers and broadcasters provide an on-line news service. Governments and other institutions use the Internet to provide an on-line service.

The Internet is an ideal medium for providing up-to-the-minute information. News, financial information and the information national and local government wishes to disseminate can be accessed on a worldwide basis. Restricting access to the Internet is difficult if not impossible so the web is itself instrumental in breaking down barriers of secrecy and state censorship.

All of the world's major newspapers have an on-line edition. If a regular *Daily Telegraph* reader is travelling abroad he or she can still 'read the *Telegraph*' without waiting for a print copy to arrive across the Atlantic. In a similar vein, if a person from Scotland is on a business trip to the USA there is no need to miss out on the news from Radio Scotland. Radio Scotland's on-line service can be accessed from the British Broadcasting Corporation (BBC) website.

Information about finance and the financial state of companies needs to be as accurate and as up-to-date as possible. Those selling stocks and shares work on a minute-by-minute basis. The Internet provides the ability to access breaking financial news, stock markets across the world and the thoughts of analysts. News agencies such as Reuters and Associated Press provide regular financial and mainstream news, as do many of the world's stock markets.

Due to its ability to provide up-to-the-minute information, official bodies have been quick to grasp the use of the Internet in providing information to the public. National, regional and local government bodies across the globe have their own websites. Pan-national organizations, including the European Union, NAFTA (North American Free Trade Association), ASEAN (Association of South East Asian Nations) and the Organization of American States (OAS), have a number of websites providing information about their policies and services.

On-line shopping

See **e-commerce**.

On-line voting

O

In recent years considerable interest has been shown in the concept of on-line voting. **Internet Service Providers (ISPs)** such as AOL have used on-line voting to ascertain subscribers' views about issues but now governments are becoming interested.

In the developed world participation in the political process is declining, with a drop in the percentage of the population actually voting being seen in most countries where voting is not compulsory. If proper safeguards to protect against impersonation and multiple vote casting can be devised, it is hoped that allowing people to vote on-line from home or a shopping centre or a doctor's surgery etc. might increase participation.

For on-line voting to work the safeguards need to be huge and there is a need to have much of the population connected to the Internet, as is happening in more and more parts of the world.

Open Source Software

A type of software source code which is freely distributed to help develop the software and or allow for customization with the software.

Operating systems

The very earliest computers were devoid of the hard disks and even monitors that are the norm today. In order to start up the hardware it had to be **booted** from an external source (derived from 'pulling it up by the bootstraps) by adding an operating system to the small amount of resident instructions.

As an internal hard disk became the norm it was necessary to develop what we now know as **DOS** (Disk Operating System) software to manage the computer system. DOS has had competitors, notably OS/2, but the world appears to have accepted DOS as the standard. The development of computer networks and the importance of communication between machines predicated the adoption of a common standard. The operating system is software that enables the user to interact with the computer. The operating system controls the computer storage, communications and task management functions. Examples of common operating stems include MS-DOS, MacOS, Linux, Windows® XP, OS2.

Optical Mark Reader (OMR)

Optical Mark Readers are often used to process questionnaires or for the automatic scoring of multiple-choice tests. OMR is a system that gathers information by using a hardware device that detects a reflection or an absence of reflection from a card or piece of paper. OMR enables the processing of hundreds or thousands of documents every hour automatically. The UK National Lottery purchase machines use OMR to record the numbers selected by the player.

Once the card or form has been completed it can be fed into a system that grades and/or gathers the information from the card. OMR systems can process up to 6000 documents per hour, far more quickly (and more accurately) than a person could ever do it. OMRs are used in education for quick and accurate marking of multiple choice papers.

Output devices

Any device such as a printer, plotter etc. that receives the output from a computer system. Further details can be found under the headings for each device.

Overload

Term used to describe when a device or service exceeds its recommended limits. For example, a popular network may become overloaded with users or a power supply may become overloaded when a surge occurs. Often when an overload occurs the device or service performs poorly or crashes.

O

Pagers

Mainly superseded by mobile telephones, pagers were one of the first mobile texting devices. Originally purely a radio device that allowed a base station to send an audible signal to the user, later versions allowed text messages to be sent. The major drawback to a pager was that, unlike a telephone, it is a one-way means of communication and for text messages the user needed to contact a central control facility and dictate the text.

Parallel

Action that is performed at the same time as another – for example, a communication that sends multiple bits of data each second.

Parallel port

Faster than a serial port but slower than a **USB**, parallel ports have traditionally been used for printer connections and memory card readers. Whilst computers still contain a parallel port, their use is rapidly being superseded by USB.

Parallel processing

In general anything that happens in **parallel** will be quicker than as a **serial** event. Parallel processing is a method of evenly distributing computer processes between two or more computer processors. This requires a computer with two or more processors installed and enabled, an operating system capable of supporting two or more processors, and a software program capable of evenly distributing processes between the computer processors. The more processors there are working at the task *at the same time*, the faster computations can be undertaken.

Not everything can happen in parallel as many mathematical functions and a large number of manufacturing processes etc. require actions that are sequential. Nevertheless, the more parallel processing that can be undertaken, the quicker the task will be accomplished.

Passwords

Passwords have been in use long before modern ICT came on the scene. A password is a set of secret characters or words utilized to gain access to a computer, network resource or data. Passwords help ensure that computers and/or data be accessible only by those who have been granted the right to view or access them. It is self-evident that passwords must be protected. Many systems use multiple passwords and/or **PIN numbers** to increase security. Those choosing passwords should avoid the obvious as there are programs that can run through millions of alternatives in order to crack a password. Names of family members etc. make very poor passwords. Passwords should never be written down – there have been cases of passwords being taped to the insides of drawers!

Patches

A patch is a piece of software code that can be applied after software has been installed to correct a problem with that program. Many software programs will have several patches released after the initial release; they commonly either update the user's version of the program or are used to solve a problem or **bug** that has been discovered. Patches are usually downloaded from the software developer's or the device producer's website.

PayPal

PayPal operate a company that allows any business or consumer with an email address and a credit card to securely, conveniently and cost-effectively send and receive payments on-line. The PayPal network builds on the existing financial infrastructure of bank accounts and credit cards to create a global, **real-time** payment solution. PayPal works across national boundaries and is useful for those organizations such as voluntary groups that have not the facilities to accept direct payment by credit card. The costs of setting up payment by credit/debit card to the receiving party can be quite considerable and only worthwhile if there are to be a large number of transactions. Once an individual has set up an account he or she can arrange a payment into that account that can then be accessed by the person for whom the money is intended. PayPal can (and is) used for sending monetary gifts across

P

the world in addition to its obvious commercial applications. The system can also be used from web-enabled mobile phones.

PDA

See **computer systems – PDA.**

PDF (Portable Data File)

PDF is a type of file, developed by Adobe, that enables users to capture the format and overall appearance of a document and have that viewed exactly the same and printed exactly the same as any other computer with a PDF viewer. The Adobe software is freely available and is often offered free of charge by those sending PDF files. Such files have the **file extension**.pdf.

PDF files cannot usually be edited by the user but do have the advantage that they are **WYSIWYG** (What You See Is What You Get) and are thus useful for manuals and e-books as the print-out accurately reflects the intention of the person setting up the file.

Peripherals

Any device that is attached to the **CPU** (central processing unit) is known as a peripheral. These include:

- External **diskette** drives
- External **CD/DVD** readers and writers
- **Zip** drives
- **Jaz** drives
- **Docking** stations
- **Scanners**
- **Plotters**
- **Printers**
- External **modems**
- **Mouse**
- **Trackerballs**

Many peripherals will require a **driver** before they can be used. The introduction of **USB** ports has made the use of peripherals much easier as many can operate in a **plug and play** mode. The vast majority of computer peripherals are incapable of operating by themselves and rely on the computer to properly function. There are a number of printers designed for use with **digital cameras** that can operate both independently and with a computer, being equipped with software that allows a degree of editing and **photo manipulation** in addition to the printing function.

PERL

PERL is an acronym for Practical Extraction and Reporting Language. It is a commonly used language in writing **CGI** scripts and programming for Internet and **web page** applications.

Phishing

Phishing, pronounced 'fishing', is the act of sending an **email** falsely claiming to be an established legitimate enterprise such as a bank etc. in an attempt to persuade the user into surrendering private information such as account numbers that will be used for identity theft. The email directs the user to visit a website where they are asked to update personal information, such as passwords and credit card, social security and bank account numbers, that the legitimate organization already has. In 2004 banks in the UK were warning **Internet banking** customers of such a 'scam' operating and warning them not to provide any such information. Phishing, also referred to as brand spoofing or carding, is a variation on 'fishing', the idea being that bait is thrown out in the hope that while most will ignore the temptation there will be those users who do in fact bite and reveal information that may be of use to a fraudster.

Photo manipulation

The process of importing an image, generally by scanning that image, and using a software program to improve the overall look of the picture or the subject in the picture. A great example of this would be removing 'red-eye' from a portrait photograph using flash photograph.

It used to be said that 'the camera never lies'. In the era of photo manipulation this is no longer true as people can be added or removed and even expressions changed. Photo manipulation uses special programs such as Adobe Photoshop or Arcsoft Photostudio, copies of which are usually included with scanners and digital cameras.

P

PIN numbers

In order for any computerized system to be effective it has to recognize the person who is making the input, query, transaction etc. It is also important to ensure that the person has the authority to do what he or she wants to do. What is required is a unique identification system that represents one individual and nobody else. Surname and forename are not enough as there is every likelihood that these are held by somebody else. How many John Smiths or Alan McDonalds are there in the UK? Very many. Name, address and post (zip in the USA) code are more specific but there could well be two people with the same name at an address. The only completely unique method of identifying a customer so that they are not confused with somebody else is to give them a Personal Identification Number (PIN) and a **password**. With ten digits (0–9) to choose from and the ability to repeat numbers, there are literally millions of possible combinations, allowing each customer to have their own unique number which can be entered into the computer or encoded onto the magnetic strip on a credit or other type of card. In the case of cards there is no password protection and recent developments have focused on adding fingerprint recognition as an added safeguard. It is unlikely that both a PIN number and a password could be guessed by a third party unless the user was very regular in his or her habits. Unfortunately too many people used to tape their password to the inside of a drawer. It should go without saying that PIN numbers should not be kept next to items to which they relate nor given to anybody else at all.

The ability of computers to recognize PIN numbers and read information off cards has been one of the truly remarkable technological discoveries of the modern age. A large number of PIN numbers consist of just 4 digits that must also be linked to either a name or a coded piece of information on a card. Take, for example, the case of an **ATM** card. Most of these use a 4-digit code. To obtain money the card must be inserted in the ATM which then reads the information on the card. The cardholder has then to, in effect, confirm the information on the card by inputting the PIN number. Only if the inputted digits match those encoded into the card will cash be dispensed. The chances of a matching PIN number being put in by chance are infinitesimally small. If fingerprint or iris recognition is included, fraudulent use is much reduced although there is always the danger that coercion will be used!

If the PIN number is revealed then the security of any system will be compromised. It will not be long before other identifiers are brought into common use. Only a few years ago the idea of reading palm prints or eyeball patterns seemed far-fetched and belonging to the world of science fiction but the former is precisely how the INPASS system introduced by the USA in the 1990s worked. Regular foreign visitors to the USA could register, undergo an FBI check and then have their palm print recorded for inclusion on an INPASS card. The card was read at special terminals at specified airports and if all the information checked out, the visitor was admitted without the need to go through immigration. Needless to say, the system was suspended after the horrific terrorist attacks of 11 September, 2001.

The credit card industry in the UK is introducing **chip and PIN** cards in order to reduce the fraudulent use of cards (see under **chip and PIN**).

PIN pads should comply with the standards set by the Royal National Institute for the Blind and have a raised dot on the number 5 key (as should telephones).

Pixels

Short for picture element, each light sensor on a digital camera produces one pixel. The more pixels, the greater the resolution. Pixels are used to specify display/monitor resolutions.

Plotters

Plotters are used to produce accurate drawings, especially for printed circuits, building and engineering projects.

A pen is held in a holder that can move in one direction while being held in an arm that moves at 90 degrees to it. The pen can be lifted from the paper by an electromagnet. Using high-precision electric motors to move the holder and the arm, very fine nibs and high quality inks, extremely accurate drawings can be produced. Plotters are often used to record the output from Computer Aided Design (**CAD**) programs.

Plug and Play (PnP)

Plug and Play is the ability of a computer to detect and configure a new piece of hardware automatically, without the user having to physically configure the hardware device. Plug and Play was introduced on IBM-compatible computers with the release of Microsoft Windows® 95 whereas Apple Macintosh computers have always supported the ability to automatically detect and install hardware.

For Plug and Play to operate properly on IBM-compatible computers the user must have the following:

- **BIOS** supporting Plug and Play.
- Windows® 95 or later (or other operating systems supporting Plug and Play).
- **Peripheral** with Plug and Play support.

P

All of today's new computers have PnP capabilities although it may still be necessary to install the necessary drivers. **USB** ports have aided the use of Plug and Play devices as they make it very easy to link them to the computer, and the use of **hubs** removes the need to keep linking and unlinking a device as ports become available.

Plug-ins

Plug-ins are software add-ons that are installed on to a program, enabling it to perform additional features. **Internet** browsers allow users to install plug-ins into the **browser** – **Flash** and **Adobe Acrobat** Reader (for viewing Portable Digital Files – **PDF**) being examples.

Pop-ups

Pop-ups, not to be confused with **Pop-up menus**, are small secondary displays, often carrying advertising or superfluous material, that appear in front of **web pages**. Some designers use pop-ups in a benign manner when they want to draw the viewer's attention to a particular function of the site. See also **spam** pop-ups. Many Internet Service Providers (ISPs) provide a pop-up blocking function so that the user can decide whether or not to allow pop-ups.

Pop-up menu

A pop-up menu is one that only appears on the screen when it is called up by the user. Windows® makes considerable use of such menus as part of the **WIMP** (Windows, Icons, Menus, Pointer) concept. Menus free the user from needing to know a whole range of commands. In a program such as Word® a series of menus are accessed from the various toolbars. All the user needs to do is point and click and the menu will be displayed. Further pointing and clicking on the menu will bring up either another related menu or cause an action to be carried out, as in the example sequence shown in Figures 36–41 (illustrating how to adjust document line spacing).

POP (Post Office Protocol)

A protocol used to retrieve **email** from a **mail server**. Most email applications use POP **protocol**, although some can use the newer **IMAP (Internet Message Access Protocol)**.

Once a message has been sent to a recipient it will be sent into the web to the recipient's domain; it will be stored in a POP (Post Office

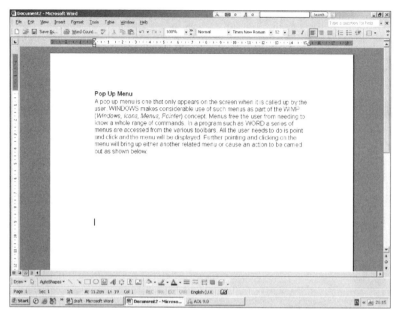

Figure 36   Pop-up menu 1: example of text with single-line spacing

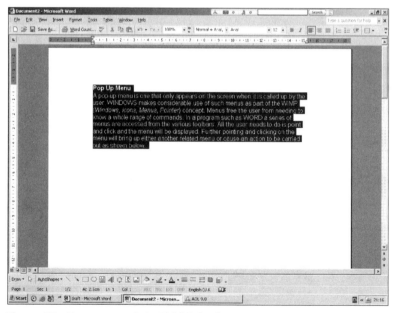

Figure 37   Pop-up menu 2: text highlighted

Click on Format

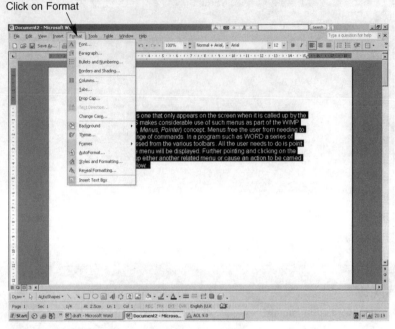

Figure 38　Pop-up menu 3: format menu pop-up

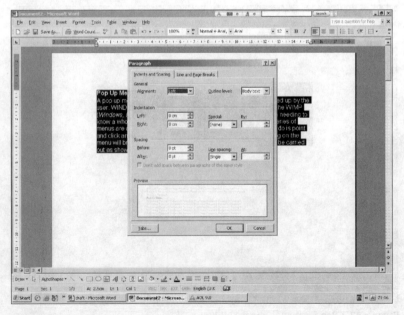

Figure 39　Pop-up menu 4: paragraph menu pop-up after clicking on paragraph on the format menu

Click on line spacing

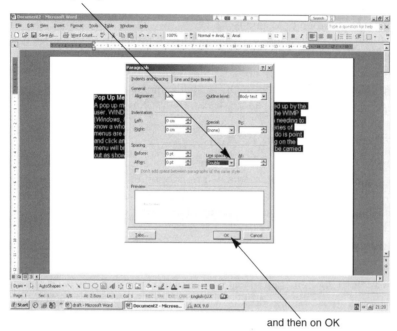

and then on OK

Figure 40   Pop-up menu 5: indents and spacing menu

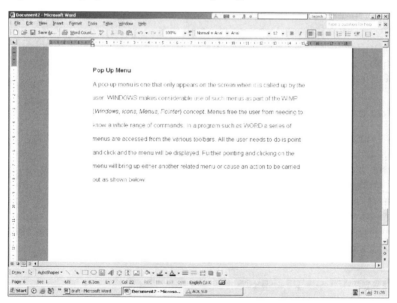

Figure 41   Pop-up menu 6: spacing changed to double-line spacing

Protocol) server where it will be held until the recipient logs on to his or her **ISP** and receives the message 'you have mail' (or its equivalent); the message can then be opened.

If the message cannot be delivered it will be returned to the sender with an indication of why delivery was impossible. The two main reasons for non-delivery are incorrect addressing and deliberate filtering. Many email systems (AOL is an example) allow users to reject messages from specified addresses as a way of avoiding spam.

Power On Self Test (POST)

The computer POST tests the computer to ensure that it meets the necessary system requirements before booting up. If the computer fails the POST the computer then returns a beep code indicating what is causing the computer not to operate in the correct manner.

Power supplies – dual voltage

While much of the world operates on 220–50 volts alternating current (AC), the USA and Canada in particular use 110–25 volts AC. Most domestic and business desktop computers use a power supply of no more than 15 volts direct current (DC). The power supply packs for modern computers and peripherals (these also use low DC voltages) are designed to convert input voltages of between 110 and 250 AC to the required low DC voltage without the need for separate 110–25 and 220–50 AC adaptors. More and more domestic appliances now use this form of inbuilt technology, allowing razors, hairdryers, mobile telephone chargers etc. to be used across the world without the need for a series of voltage adaptor

Power supplies – stability

Although voltage adaptors provide for a fairly stable power supply, sudden surges of power or the effects of electrical storms on telephone lines leading to **modems** can cause damage to sensitive electronic components. Modems and power lines can be protected cheaply and easily by installing surge protectors that ensure stability of supply. In areas where power supplies may be problematic, a sensible precaution is to install a backup power supply independent of the mains, configured to kick in automatically if the mains power fails.

Presentation packages

See **applications/software – presentation packages**.

Printers

The printers attached to ICT systems are now very sophisticated and provide even the domestic user with the ability to produce high quality hard copy using colour where necessary. Printers fall into different types, as listed below.

Printers – dot matrix

Dot matrix printers are the oldest and least sophisticated in current use. The term 'dot matrix' refers to the process of placing dots of ink from a series of pins to form an image, the quality of the image being determined by the number of dots per inch. Dot matrix printers were first introduced by Centronics in 1970 and are a type of printer that uses print heads to shoot ink or strike an ink ribbon to place hundreds to thousands of little dots to form text and/or images. When introduced, the dot matrix printer enabled cheap although low quality printing for even the smallest computer user. Nowadays dot matrix printers are not commonly used because of the low quality print-outs when compared to **inkjet printers** or other later printer technologies. Many early dot matrix printers used paper with sprocket holes (continuous listing paper) and ribbon-style ink cartridges. These were useful for printing out programs or accounts but less applicable to business documents. Graphics were a problem area for dot matrix printers and they were confined to single-colour printing.

An alternative technology used by the UK firm of Amstrad for its dedicated PCW word processor employed daisy wheel-type heads that could be interchanged to give different fonts.

Printers – laser

First developed at Xerox PARC in 1971, a laser printer is a type of printer that utilizes laser technology to print images on the paper. The laser recreates the image on a negatively charged drum which will then collect toner that is positively charged to attract to the areas of the image. The paper is then negatively charged, so that the positively charged toner is attracted to the paper and then is fused onto the paper.

Laser printers produce a high-quality print. Initially only black, white and grey were possible but there are now laser colour printers that use colour toner cartridges (usually black + cyan, magenta and yellow). One of the downsides of a laser printer is that the toner used (similar to that used in photocopiers) needs to be disposed of in an environmentally friendly manner, especially as huge quantities are consumed daily across the globe.

P

Printers – inkjet

Inkjet printers form letters and images by spraying streams of quick-drying ink onto paper. The ink is stored in a disposable ink cartridge. This type of printer is certainly the most popular for domestic use as it is easy to use and capable of fairly high speed, good quality printing and can print in colour. Though the purchase price is quite low, the consumption of ink cartridges can be high especially when used to print out photographs. Inkjet printers can be small enough to be battery powered and even, as Sharp did a number of years ago, built into a **laptop computer**. As with **dot matrix printers** it is the number of dots per inch that define the quality of printing although even the cheapest inkjet printer is capable of far higher density of print than a dot matrix printer.

Printers – multifunction

Multifunction printers combine a printing, copier and fax facility in one machine, often using colour inkjet technology. Multifunction printers are especially useful in the small office or home office environment as they are relatively inexpensive to purchase and combine a number of functions within the same **footprint**. They are not designed, however, for high volume copying and printing.

Printers – photographic

The advent of **digital** photography has led to a need for printers that can produce high quality photographic images in colour. No longer does a camera user have to send a film away; he or she can print out the photographs at home. If a printer is not available there are plenty of retailers who will download photographs from the camera and print them out.

The most basic of inkjet printers can be used for photographic printing using special photographic paper. Photographs made up of **pixels** (such as **digital** photographs) do need high-resolution printing if they are to be sharp and clear.

It is possible to buy specialist photographic printers that work using dyer sublimation, a process whereby dyes are heated to vaporize the ink which then sublimates onto the paper. This produces a much more continuous tone on the photograph, albeit at a higher cost.

Another alternative is to use thermo-autochrome printing. This technique uses heat and light on special paper and requires no toner or cartridges.

P

Processor architecture

The term 'architecture' is usually used when referring to the internal structure of a processor. The integrated circuits that make up a processor contain a variety of modules: registers, counters, memory elements, logic and arithmetic units etc. An instruction set contains all the instructions that are available for use with a particular processor.

Programmable ROM (PROM)

Programmable Read Only Memory is a type of computer memory chip capable of being programmed. Once the PROM has been programmed the information written is permanent and cannot be erased or deleted.

Programs

A program is a software application designed to run on a computer and to provide the instructions for the computer to carry out tasks. Without programs the computer may 'work' but is unable to be used to carry out tasks.

Many program **files** on IBM-compatible computers commonly end with a **file extension** of .bat, .exe, .com, or .pif. Executing these files will commonly open the program.

'To program' or 'programming' are terms used to describe the process of a programmer developing a program.

Protocols

A protocol is a standard used to define a method of exchanging data over a computer network such as local area network (LAN), wide area network (WAN), Internet, Intranet, etc. Each protocol has its own method for how data is formatted when sent and what to do with it once received; how that data is compressed; and/or how to check for errors in data.

P

Proxy server

A proxy server is a computer **server** or software **program** which is part of the gateway that separates a local network from outside networks. A proxy server will generally **cache** all pages accessed through the network. When a page is accessed that is not in the proxy server's cache the proxy server will access the page using its own **IP** address, cache the page and forward it to the user accessing that page. In doing so the proxy server improves performance as it can deliver stored pages rather than having to access the web and can also filter out any undesirable material. A proxy server can provide **firewall**, **anti-spam**, **anti-virus** and **URL** filtering for a network.

Query

In general the term 'query' is commonly used to describe a question or request that is made by a user or another computer and/or device. When referring to a database or search, a query is a field or option used to locate information within a database or other location.

Queue management software

Even with **parallel processing** the computer cannot do everything at once and jobs need to be prioritized and held. Queue management software is for holding items in a queue or buffer while other items are being processed.

R r

RAM (Random Access Memory)

The main memory of a computer. RAM, unlike ROM (Read Only Memory), can be accessed and changed by the user.

Real numbers

Real numbers are ones that actually exist, such as 2, 756, -7, etc. The reason why mathematicians need real numbers is that certain advanced mathematics need to make use of imaginary numbers such as 'I' which is $\sqrt{-1}$. Minus one or indeed any minus number cannot have a square root as minus times minus always gives a plus. The $\sqrt{25}$ is 5, and 5 * 5 = 25 but the $\sqrt{-25}$ cannot be -5 because -5 * -5 = +25 not -25. Illogical as it might seem, such imaginary numbers are important in mathematics.

Real time

Real time is used to describe a process or event that occurs immediately. For example, the majority of all chat programs occur in real time, where messages are seen immediately after the user presses his or her enter key. **Webcams** allow users to obtain real-time imagery from a huge number of locations.

Real-time processing

A real-time operating system is a computer operating system designed to handle events as they occur. Real-time operating systems are commonly found and used in robotics, complex multimedia and animation, communications, and have various military and government uses.

Registry (Microsoft Windows®)

The registry contains extended information, settings and various other values for the Microsoft Windows® operating systems. Within the registry the user can control much of the operating system as well as solve any issues with Windows®. The computer registry consists of two files hidden in the Windows® directory, system.dat and user.dat. User-specific system information is contained in the user.dat file and computer- and hardware-specific information in the system.dat file.

Resolution

Resolution refers to the image quality of a printer, monitor or **digital camera**/camcorder. In monitors, the resolution is measured by the number of pixels in a given area. The higher the number of **pixels** per given area, the higher the resolution and the better the picture.

Restore

See **system restore**.

Retrieving

The term used to describe the process of searching for, locating and returning data. For example, a user may retrieve a document on a computer to be viewed or modified.

Return key

See **enter key**.

Risk analysis

Risk analysis is used to identify the degree of risk to a computer system, systems or network. Such risks include fire, failure, malicious damage, criminal and terrorist attack. Where the risk comes from a human being a perpetrator analysis is also carried out, detailing the profile of those who might wish the system harm. A key issue is whether such individuals or groups have the technical ability to achieve their objectives.

Risk analysis enables an organization to formulate policies and procedures to protect systems. Given the high degree of dependence that organizations, the military, governments and even individuals have on computer systems, risk analysis is an import part of ICT.

Even the domestic and small business user needs to carry out such an analysis. Data can be lost and for a small business this can often cause huge problems. Even simple steps such as performing regular **back-up** operations can help reduce the risk of losing everything.

R

ROM (Read Only Memory)

The memory of a computer, usually used for the operating system, that only allows the user to read from it (unlike RAM). ROM is used for permanent storage of the **BIOS** and other pieces of software installed at the time of manufacture.

RSI (Repetitive Strain Injury)

A type of injury to the joints, for example in the wrist, that is said to occur with repeated small movements over a period of time. RSI has been said to afflict those inputting data via a keyboard. Wrist supports are available to reduce the danger of RSI.

R

Safe mode

This is a software mode that enables users who use Microsoft Windows® 95 and later to enter into Windows® safely after a problem and correct any problems that may be preventing them from entering normal mode. Safe mode was first introduced in Microsoft Windows® 95.

When it enters safe mode the Windows® system only loads those parts of itself that are needed to correct problems. When booting into safe mode the lowest settings are used, including the video card. This means that the resolution is 640 x 480, 16 colours when in safe mode. Windows® indicates when a user is in safe mode by displaying 'Safe Mode' in each of the corners of the window and/or by displaying a safe mode message when first loading into Windows®. In addition the screen display will be at minimum resolution. In safe mode the user only has access to basic files and drivers (mouse, monitor, keyboard, mass storage, video, default system services, and no network connections).

Safe mode can be used to help diagnose problems. If a symptom does not reappear when starting in safe mode then default settings and minimum device drivers can be eliminated as possible causes of the problem. If a newly added device or a changed driver is causing problems safe mode (or **System restore**), can be used to remove the device or reverse the change.

Satellite communications

One of the problems with wireless communication occurs when it is used over long distances. At the beginning of the twentieth century Marconi proved that wireless (radio) could be used even when no line of sight existed and over long distances. Prior to his work it was believed that long-distance applications would not be possible due to the curvature of the earth. As it is, the charged layers in the atmosphere bounce the signal back to earth.

Unfortunately, however, such transmissions are at the mercy of atmospheric conditions. One day it is possible to pick up a transmission from Australia if it is strong enough and the next it may be difficult to hear a signal from quite near. Standard radio quality can be quite problematic as the signal strength fades over distance and this makes it an inappropriate medium for data transmission where quality and consistency are all-important.

Super high frequency radio waves (known as microwaves) can be used over long distances without loss of quality provided that there are no major obstructions. Whilst few parts of the earth are obstruction-free the line between the earth and space is. When the Russians began the satellite era in the 1950s it was realized that satellites could be used to relay microwaves from an earth transmitter to a receiver provided both were in the **footprint** of the satellite. Satellites move across the sky and thus it might be thought difficult to track them accurately. However, whilst there are medium and low earth satellites that do move relative to the earth and thus do need tracking, it is also possible to have geosynchronous satellites which move at the same speed as the earth and thus appear to maintain a fixed position and need no tracking. Tracking of non-geosynchronous satellites can be carried out automatically and they are much cheaper than their 'stationary' equivalents although their lifespan is much shorter (5–12 years as opposed to 15 years and more). Geosynchronous satellites are much further from the earth and thus they have a bigger footprint although the distance does give a time delay to any signal, as the fastest it can travel is the speed of light. This delay is known as latency.

Microwave transmission, revolutionary in the 1960s, is now a norm of communication. Satellites have enabled highly accurate navigation and positioning systems to be developed. For details see **GPS (Global Positioning Satellite)**.

Satnav

See **GPS**.

Scanners

Scanners are devices with the ability to input text, graphics and pictures into the computer using photocopier technology to scan the image and make a digital copy. Modern scanners use **USB connections**. There are three main types: flatbed, hand-held and 35mm.

Scanners – flatbed

Flatbed scanners are designed to be used for pages and photographs etc. As the name suggests, they scan in material that is in a flat format. Like many **peripherals** each type of scanner needs **device drivers**. Many computers now come with the device drivers for popular software preloaded into the computer system.

Flatbed scanner software usually includes Optical Character Recognition (**OCR**) functions that allows text to be recognized, edited and pasted into documents. A flatbed scanner may have an attachment to scan 35mm slides (see entry below).

Scanners – hand-held

It is also possible to purchase small hand-held scanners that are rolled over a picture or small piece of text. These do not have the sophistication of larger scanners.

Scanners – 35mm

35mm slides are quite small and there are dedicated scanners for these items. Such scanners are especially useful for backing up slide collections and for inputting slide copies into **presentation applications**. Although digital photography has gained in popularity, the fact that 35mm slides use blocks of colour for high resolution as opposed to **digital pixels** has ensured that the medium has survived.

Screensaver

Screensavers are software programs that become activated after the computer has been inactive for a specified amount of time. Screensavers were originally designed to help prevent images or text from being burned into older monitors. Cathode ray monitor screens are bombarded by charged electrical particles and if the pattern is not changed these can cause an image to be burnt on the screen. In order to see the power of such particles it is possible to set up a small indoor television aerial connected to a television, the assembly being placed a few metres from a computer with a cathode ray-type monitor. If both the TV and the computer are switched on at the same time the TV may well display a faint image of the computer screen over the television programme. It is these charged particles that account for the dust that accumulates on televisions and older type monitors – the dust is attracted to the static charge on the screen.

Buildings can be fitted with special coatings on the walls and windows to prevent older-type computer screens being read by people outside the building who are bent on some form of espionage.

S

Modern monitors, especially those using the **Liquid Crystal Display (LCD)** technology used today, no longer suffer from this issue and screen savers are commonly used today for entertainment, a method of protection, and/or a method of informing visitors of the computer user's status. Most computers come with a small number of screensavers pre-installed and there are many hundreds that can be downloaded from the Internet. Any graphics file folder can be used as a screensaver. The aim is to have a constantly changing image, with the time before the screen-saver activates and the time between changes being set by the user.

Scrolling

The action of moving the visual portions of a screen up, down, left or right in order to see additional information on the monitor or the next or previous pages. Scrolling can be accomplished using the 'Home', 'End', 'Page Up' and 'Page Down' keys on the **keyboard** or by clicking on the scroll bar at the right-hand side of a window or by using the scroll wheel on a *mouse* that is so equipped.

SCSI

Standing for Small Computer System Interface, SCSI is one of the commonly used interfaces for disk drives. It is a parallel interface that transfers information at the rate of eight bits per second and faster.

Search agents

Search agents scan the contents of a limited number of sites by gather-ing information from a number of them simultaneously. By performing a simultaneous search, albeit in a limited area, a search agent can save a user considerable time.

An example of a search agent is 'Metacrawler', originally developed in 1994 at the University of Washington by then graduate student Erik Selberg and Associate Professor Oren Etzioni. Metacrawler searches the **Internet**'s top **search engines**, including Google, Yahoo!, Ask Jeeves, About, Teoma, FindWhat, LookSmart. Thus it provides the user with results from the combined pool of the world's leading search engines instead of results from only one single search engine.

Search engines

The method and software used by Internet users to search for pages on the World Wide Web. Web pages are registered with the search engine databases. Yahoo!, Lycos, Excite etc. are commonly employed search engines. They are nearly always funded by advertising and are thus free to the user. Most organizations register their web pages with all of the major search engines, Yahoo!, Lycos, AltaVista, Excite, Google, Ask Jeeves etc.

Google is an important search engine used by many **Internet Service Providers (ISPs)**. At Stanford University in the USA Google's founders, Larry Page and Sergey Brin, developed a new approach to on-line searching. Google is now widely recognized as the world's largest search engine. It is an easy-to-use free service that usually returns relevant results in a fraction of a second. ('Googol' is the mathematical term coined by Milton Sirotta, nephew of American mathematician Edward Kasner, for a 1 followed by 100 zeros.)

Another important search engine is Yahoo!, an organization whose history is illustrative of how the **Internet** has grown. Yahoo! began as a scientific hobby. The two developers of Yahoo!, David Filo and Jerry Yang, doctoral candidates in Electrical Engineering at Stanford University in California, started their guide to the World Wide Web in April 1994 as a way to keep track of their personal interests on the Internet. They soon found that their lists were becoming too long and unwieldy. They began to spend more and more time on the search engine that became Yahoo!

During 1994 they converted Yahoo! into a customized database designed to serve the needs of the thousands of users who began to use the service through the closely bound academic and Internet communities both in the US and later abroad. They therefore developed software to help them locate, identify and edit material stored on the Internet efficiently. The name Yahoo! is supposed to stand for 'Yet Another Hierarchical Officious Oracle' but Filo and Yang insist they selected the name because they considered themselves Yahoos! The Yahoo! database at first resided on Yang's student workstation, while the search engine was lodged on Filo's computer. In 1995 Filo and Yang were invited to move their files over to larger computers housed at Netscape Communications, one of the early entrants into **browser** provision. Today's commercial version of Yahoo! contains organized information on tens of thousands of computers linked to the Web.

The fact that from early on Yahoo! was used by those not in the USA has meant a rapid global growth for the organization. As an example, there are Yahoo! organizational offices and Internet access in Denmark, France, Germany, Italy, Norway, Spain, Sweden, UK/Eire, Australia, New Zealand, China/Hong Kong, India, Japan, South Korea, Singapore,

Taiwan, Argentina, Brazil, Canada, Mexico, and of course the USA (where the sites can be accessed in Spanish or Chinese). Yahoo! is no longer a hobby but a global organization that shows what is possible in a very short space of time given a couple of entrepreneurs and a vision.

Sector

Disks, CDs etc. are subdivided into sectors. A sector is the smallest addressable unit on a storage device.

Secure electronic transaction (SET)

Developed by the credit-card operators Mastercard and Visa, SET places greater emphasis on the validation by both the parties to the transaction than does **secure socket layer (SSL)**. SET uses digital signatures to ensure the validity of the card user.

Knott, G. and Waits, N. (2000), *Information and Communication Technology* (Sunderland: Business Education Publishers).

Secure servers

In order for e-commerce to prosper those using it, especially customers, need to know that their transactions are secure and that the details of their credit cards are safe. **Protocols** have been developed by banks and credit card companies in a variety of areas. One of the most important of these is the secure **server** that guarantees that the transaction has been handled in a secure manner. See also **SET**, **SSL** and **encryption**. Secure servers indicate to the customer that he or she is linked to such a server – this is usually carried out when the customer is about to enter credit card details.

Secure socket layer (SSL)

The standard means of ensuring security between client **browsers** and Internet **servers**.

See also **SET**.

Semiconductor

Materials that have the properties of an insulator when pure or at low temperature but those of a conductor at higher temperatures or when containing impurities. Semiconductors are commonly used and found in almost all electronic devices. Examples of semiconductor materials are germanium, selenium and silicon. These materials are then treated (known as doped) to create an excess or lack of electrons. This allows the device to control the amplification/modulate or switching of an electronic signal. Computer chips, both for the **central processing unit (CPU)** and **memory**, are composed of semiconductor materials. Semiconductors make it possible to miniaturize electronic components, such as transistors. Not only does miniaturization mean that the components take up less space, it also means that they are faster and require less energy and thus produce less heat.

Serial

Term used to describe the process of transmitting information one bit at a time or sequentially.

Server

A server is either a computer or a device on a network that manages the network's resources. A file server is a computer and storage device dedicated to the task of storing files, so that any user on the network can store and retrieve files on the server. A print server is a computer that manages one or more printers, and a network server is a computer that manages the traffic on the network. A database server is a computer system that processes database queries. Servers are often dedicated, i.e. they perform no other tasks besides their server function.

On a large network servers may take up considerable space and require large numbers of connections. The 'Blade Server' from IBM seeks to simplify the network server. Blade servers are slim, hot-swappable devices that fit into a single chassis bay rather like books in a bookshelf. Whilst each is an independent server, with its own processors, memory, storage, network controllers, operating system and applications, it fits into the chassis and plugs into a mid- or backplane and shares power, fans, **diskette** etc. drives, switches and ports with other blade servers, thus freeing up space.

Servlet

This is a **Java** program that runs as part of a network service, usually an **HTTP server** and responds to requests from clients.

The most common use for a servlet is to extend a web server by generating web content dynamically. For instance, a user may require information from a **database**. A servlet can be written that receives the request, gets and processes the data as needed by the user and then returns the result.

SET mechanisms

Standing for Secure Electronic Transaction, SET was developed by credit card companies as a secure means of facilitating credit card transactions across the Internet. SET places greater emphasis on the validation by both parties when compared to **SSL**.

Setup

Setup describes the overall process of connecting and preparing a software program, hardware device and/or computer to properly function. A file commonly named setup.exe is executed to begin the process of installing a software program onto a computer. Most users do not have to worry about the mechanics of setup as the vast majority of software applications have a **wizard** that carries out most of the procedure automatically.

Shareware

Software distributed for evaluation without cost, but that requires payment to the author for full rights. If, after trying the software, you do not intend to use it, you simply delete it. Using unregistered shareware beyond the evaluation period is pirating.

Silicon/Silicon chip

Silicon (chemical symbol Si) was first isolated and described as an element by the Swedish Chemist Jöns Jacob Berzelius in 1824.

Silicon is a non-metallic chemical element in the carbon family and is the second most abundant element in the earth's crust. Silicon does not occur uncombined in nature. Sand and almost all rocks contain silicon combined with oxygen, forming silica. When silicon combines with other elements, such as iron, aluminium or potassium, a silicate is formed.

Silicon is the basic material used to make computer chips, **transistors** and other electronic circuits and switching devices as the nature of its atomic structure makes the element an ideal **semiconductor**.

Silicon is commonly 'doped' or mixed with other elements, such as boron, phosphorous and arsenic, to alter its conductive properties. A silicon chip is an **integrated circuit** made primarily of silicon.

SIM card

Part of mobile telephone technology, a SIM (Subscriber Identity Module) is a **microchip** card around the size of a postage stamp. It is a key element in over 600 million GSM (Global System for Mobile) mobile phones – representing about 70 per cent of the global mobile handset market.

A SIM is actually a tiny computer inside the mobile telephone that has memory (for data and applications), a processor and the ability to interact with the user. Current SIMs typically have 16 to 64 KB of memory, which provides plenty of room for storing hundreds of personal phone numbers, text messages and value-added services.

As the SIM card is removable by the user, it makes it possible to carry a mobile subscription and data through different types and generations of GSM phone. The interfaces between the mobile handset and the SIM card are fully standardized and there are already specifications in place for third-generation handsets and SIMs. All that is required when upgrading a telephone is to use the SIM card from the old model to replace the one pre-installed in the new purchase. In this way lists of numbers are kept and the user also keeps his or her old mobile telephone number.

Simulations

See **applications/software – simulations.**

Skunkworks

This strange term refers to a typically small and loosely structured group of people who research and develop a project for the sake of innovation rather than its commercial possibilities. The term tends to be used in regard to technology projects. A skunkworks generally operates independent of a company's normal research and development operations and therefore often is subject to limitations in resources. Skunkworks projects often are undertaken in secret, with the understanding that if the development is successful then the product will be designed later according to the usual process. A famous example of a skunkworks project is the first Apple Macintosh computer and certain military aircraft technologies from the Lockheed Company in Georgia.

S

The term itself originated in the USA and comes from the Skonk Works, the Kickapoo Joy Juice bootleg brewing operation in Al Capp's Li'l Abner comic strip.

Smart cards

In ICT smart card can have one of two meanings:

1. When referring to a computer, a smart card is an expansion card capable of performing its own processing.
2. The term 'smart card' is used in popular speak to refer to a credit or identity card that has the capability of storing transaction data and help with improved security. Smart cards can contain embedded chips that hold personal details, retinal patterns, signature copies, finger prints etc., which can help the unique identification of an individual and his or her authorization to use the card.

As credit card fraud has increased so the card issuers have been experimenting with encoding more and more personal identification data onto their cards to ensure that incorrect use is minimized.

Smart client

Smart client is an **Internet**-connected device that allows the user's local applications to interact with server-based applications through the use of Web services. For example, a smart client running a **word processing** application can interface with a remote **database** over the Internet in order to collect **data** from the **database** to be used in the word processing document. Smart clients are distinguished by key characteristics:

- They support work **off-line** – smart clients can work with data even when they are not connected to the Internet (which distinguishes them from **browser**-based applications, which do not work when the device is not connected to the Internet).
- Smart client applications have the ability to be deployed and updated in **real time** over the **network** from a centralized server.
- Smart client applications support multiple platforms and languages because they are built on web services.
- Smart client applications can run on almost any device that can be connected to the Internet – **desktops**, **laptops**, **notebooks**, **PDAs**, and mobile telephones.

SMTP (Simple Mail Transport Protocol)

The Internet email delivery format for transmitting email messages between servers.

Sneakware

See **adware**.

Software

Software is a collection of instructions that enables a user to interact with the computer or have the computer perform specific tasks or applications for them. The vast majority of software used for applications is purchased as ready-to-use, user-friendly packages.

Sony iLink

See **Firewire interface**.

SOAP (Simple Object Access Protocol)

A messaging protocol used to encode the information in web service request and response messages before sending them over a network. SOAP messages are independent of any operating system or protocol and may be transported using a variety of Internet protocols.

SOPs (Standard Operating Procedures)

A set of laid-down rules and procedures for dealing with commonplace events in order to achieve consistency.

Spam

Spam is unrequested and unwelcome email messages and attachments sent out as advertising material in bulk. **Internet Service Providers** have been spending large sums to stop spam and routinely provide spam filters that look for emails with keywords such as 'viagara', 'XXX' etc. in them as these are often spam. In addition to the danger of spam attachments and messages containing **viruses**, they also tend to clog up inboxes and the Internet.

Spam pop-ups

Users of Windows® 2000 or XP may find that from time to time highly annoying grey advertising **pop-up** messages, headed 'Messenger Service', appear on the screen. These are 'spam pop-ups', sent by other Internet users (usually commercial enterprises) offering such things as US university degrees or adult services. These messages are sent via the Windows® Messenger Service software.

To avoid receiving such unsolicited messages the user can change the Windows® settings to disable Messenger Service.

Spreadsheets

See **applications/software – spreadsheets**.

Spyware

See **adware**.

SQL (Structured Query Language)

A language originally known as SEQUEL (Structured English QUEry Language) that was developed by IBM in the 1970s. It has become the standard database language.

Stealth virus

A computer **virus** that actively hides itself from **anti-virus software** by either masking the size of the file that it hides in or temporarily removing itself from the infected file and placing a copy of itself in another location on the drive, replacing the infected file with an uninfected one that it has stored on the **hard drive**. The ability to hide makes this type of virus very difficult to spot and remove.

S

Stemming

Search engines such as **Google** now use stemming (from the word 'stem') technology. Thus, when appropriate, they will search not only for the defined search terms, but also for words that are similar to some or all of those terms. A search for 'diabetics' dietary needs' will also search for 'diabetics' diet needs', and other related variations of the terms. Any variants of the terms that were searched for will be highlighted in the snippet of text accompanying each result.

Stock control

See applications/software – stock control.

Strategy (ICT)

Gerry Johnson and Kevin Scholes (see below) have defined strategy in terms of the direction and scope of an organization over the long term: 'ideally making a match between the organization's resources and its changing environment, and in particular its markets, customers or clients, so as to meet stakeholder expectations'.

Using this definition applied to **Information and Communications Technology**, it is possible to say that an ICT strategy is: the direction and scope of the Information and Communications technology developed by the organization for its employees and other concerned partners in order to ensure that the organization can respond to changes in its external environment.

The ICT strategy should form part of the overall strategy of the organization – it is nested within the overall strategy. Although this might seem common sense, there have been cases where the ICT provided has not been linked to the overall strategy. Considerable quantities of ICT have been provided, often at considerable cost but with little connection to what the organization needs.

The key question that needs to be asked is: 'How will this ICT provision further the objectives of the organization?' This can then be further considered in terms of how the ICT will:

- help cut costs;
- help gain extra revenue;
- give the organization a competitive advantage over its competitors;
- assist in gaining and retaining customers;
- allow the organization to develop new products and services;
- improve relationships with suppliers.

If it appears that the proposed strategy will benefit the organization, it is then necessary to think about:

- capital costs;
- on-going costs;
- security;
- the need to train staff (and the costs associated with this).

These components form the planning stage. At this stage it is vital that not only ICT professionals are involved but also the users. The earlier users are involved the less likely it is that there will be resistance from the work force to any changes that are made. Since the beginnings of widespread computer use there have been fears that jobs will be lost. Involving people in the formulation of the strategy is a good way to begin to address such fears. The ICT needs of the organization in terms of the support and opportunities ICT provides are one factor (a very important one) in defining the ICT strategy but so are the needs of the individual user. Who better to know a user's needs than the user? ICT strategy formulation should always include user input.

Strategy is about planning for the future; tactics are concerned with the day-to-day implementation of strategy. Not only does there need to be a strategy for the plan but there also needs to be an overall strategy for how the plan will be implemented and monitored.

A new ICT strategy may require new equipment and cabling. How is this to be managed? Will there be periods when the ICT provision is reduced as a result of making the changes and what effect will this have on operations? Without naming the organizations concerned, there has been more than one instance of an IT department carrying out cabling work without prior notification to users. The results of this can be lost business, and very often a customer who leaves never comes back. If users know in advance what is happening, why it is happening and when it will happen they can make alternative provision and the problems will be reduced.

The final step is to consider how the strategy will be monitored and evaluated. At the very beginning the performance criteria for the strategy need to be set in very precise terms:

'The strategy will have been a success if' (for example):

- costs have been reduced by X amount; or
- the time to complete task Y has been reduced; or
- business has increased by Z.

All too often somebody has an idea which they think will help the organization. 'If we upgrade to a particular system then we will do better.' The premiss may be true but ICT, like all other aspects of an organization's activities, needs to pay its way either by aiding profits or improving service (not all organizations operate on a for-profit basis, for example local government etc.).

The process is cyclical not linear. The cycle can be represented as shown in Figure 42.

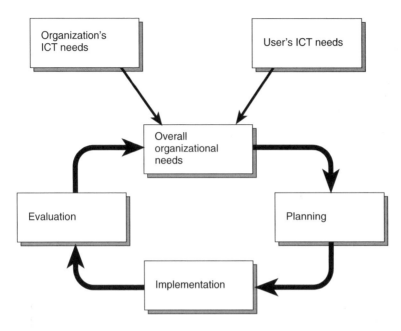

Figure 42   The strategic cycle

Johnson, G. and Scholes, K. (2004), *Exploring Corporate Strategy*, 7th edn (London: Financial Times, Prentice Hall).

Streaming

Streaming is a technique for transferring data such that it can be processed as a steady and continuous stream. Streaming technologies are becoming increasingly important with the growth of the **Internet** because most users do not have fast enough access to download large **multimedia** video/audio files quickly. With streaming, the user's **browser** or **plug-in** can start displaying the data before the entire file has been transmitted.

For streaming to work, the user receiving the data must be able to collect the data and send it as a steady stream to the application that is processing the data and converting it to sound or pictures. This means that if the streaming client receives the data more quickly than required, it needs to save the excess data in a **buffer**. If the data does not come quickly enough, however, the presentation of the data will not be smooth. A file that is streaming will indicate that it is 'buffering'. Small fragments of the file will play until the whole file is transferred and then the file will run. If the file is a video file this means that snippets of video will be seen, followed by the whole piece.

Tape streaming is the movement of data to magnetic tapes and is covered under its own heading.

Strings

A string is any series of characters that does not have a clear mathematical meaning, e.g. WSH56P2 or indeed any word. Dates show some attributes of both numbers and strings – see above under **dates**.

Subroutines

A subroutine is a self-contained routine, encoded once and then available to be called up at any time within the running of the main routine. Once the subroutine has been executed control reverts to the main routine.

Surfing

Surfing is a slang term originating in the USA that refers to the act of a user browsing the Internet by going from one page to another page using **hyperlinks**. Rather as a surfer allows the surf to carry him or her in a general direction, so an Internet surfer allows the links to transport him or her through different sites. The surfer may have little idea of where he or she wants to go. Unlike a serious search, surfing is almost a pastime.

SVGA (Super Video Graphics Array)

A set of video standards that is replacing **VGA (Video Graphics Array)**. SVGA monitors are capable of displaying up to 16 million colours with a resolution of 800 x 600 on 14-inch monitors or up to a 1200 x 1600 resolution on a 20-inch monitor.

Synchronization

Sometimes referred to as clocking, synchronization is a term used to describe the process of hardware devices or computers connecting to each other and making the information identical to what is on the other system or hardware device. A good example of synchronization is when the computer synchronizes the time with another computer or hardware device. **Personal Digital Assistants (PDAs)** require synchronization software to pass data to and from themselves and the user's PC. Instead of moving data one file at a time (a laborious process) the two devices can be set to synchronize automatically.

Synergy

A phenomenon where the sum of the parts is greater than the whole. A computer and a camera connected to a telephone can aid communication far more than might be expected by examining the individual capabilities of the three components. Synergy between components has been the factor that has led to the exponential growth of ICT. The linkage of these components within a network has meant an ever-increasing use of technology not just to process information but to transmit it swiftly across the globe and to link not only computers but the human brains of the decision makers and planners within organizations. A computer on its own is a powerful tool, as is a telephone. Put them together and link them to other computers and telephones and their power increases many fold.

System configuration

See config.sys

System Restore

Also **restore**, System Restore is a term used to describe the process of reverting a computer back to its original configuration. Windows® has a very easy-to-use system restore function (see Figure 43).

System Restore can be used to undo harmful changes to the computer and restore its settings and performance. System Restore returns the computer to an earlier time (called a restore point) without causing the user to lose recent work, such as saved documents, **email**, or **history** and **favourites** lists. Any new software or upgrades added since the last checkpoint will, however, be lost.

Any changes that System Restore makes to the computer are completely reversible. The computer automatically creates restore points (called system checkpoints), but the user can also use System Restore to create his or her own restore points. If the user encounters a software problem, restoring the computer to a date and time when it was known to be running properly may well solve the problem.

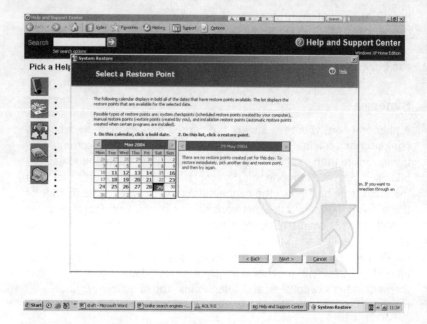

Figure 43 System restore – highlighted dates indicate system checkpoints

S

Tape streaming

Magnetic tape (similar to that used in tape recorders) formed an early method of data storage. Although largely superseded by magnetic discs (**diskettes, Zip** and **Jaz**) and by **CDs** and **DVDs**, in many instances large companies still use such tape to back-up very large amounts of data. Tape drives are capable of backing up a couple of hundred megabytes to several gigabytes of information without having to spend large sums of money on disks as the tape cartridges are relatively inexpensive. Their major disadvantage is the speed at which they back-up and recover information. Tape drives are sequential access devices, which means that to read any data on the tape drive, the tape drive must read all preceding data. The process of transferring the data to tape is known as tape streaming.

Telecommuting

Working from a remote base (including the individual's home), linked to the rest of the organization via telephone and computer.

See **home-working**.

Teleconferencing

Often used before videoconferencing, teleconferencing uses telephones rather than video to link a group of participants. Although easier to set up, teleconferencing does not provide participants with visual clues.

Telecottage

A central point, usually in a remote area, that is equipped with ICT facilities and which acts as a base for a group of home workers or trainees. The telecottage can provide the necessary telephone lines and ICT technical support in a more cost-effective manner than providing it for an individual. It also provides a social context for home-working/telecommuting to operate within – there can be social tea breaks.

Telephone technologies

Telephone technology is a key ingredient in ICT. Invented by Alexander Graham Bell at the end of the nineteenth century, the telephone is now a standard feature in nearly every home in the developed world and every business worldwide. It is a piece of equipment often taken for granted and yet it lies at the heart of the communications and computer revolution.

Even in the 1950s most telephone calls in the UK were made either from business premises or from a public call box; the domestic telephone, although gaining in popularity, was not installed in the majority of homes. By the year 2000 the telephone had become a fixture in nearly every house in the developed world, with many people owning two or three land-line telephones plus a mobile telephone. The telephone is possibly one of the great icons of the later twentieth century and when, from the 1980s onwards, it became possible to link computers using telephone lines, whole new possibilities of communication and business were opened up. **ATMs** rely on a telephone link to a central computer to carry out the transaction with the customer; without the telephone this would be impossible.

The basic workings of a telephone system are relatively simple. A number of instruments that can both transmit and receive the human voice are connected either by wires or radio to a central switching point, where the message is routed to the desired other receiver transmitter. Originally the switching of calls was a manual task with switchboard operators plugging wires into the relevant sockets.

In the 1950s in the UK, prior to the introduction of STD (Subscriber Trunk Dialling), any calls other than local ones (which could be handled at a semi-automatic telephone exchange) required the intervention of the operator, who would connect the call. International calls needed to be booked in advance. As electronics improved, so it became possible to dial anywhere directly from home. In the UK, until the 1980s, telephony was a government monopoly – subscribers not buying but having to rent a telephone (like Henry Ford's famous Model T, you could have your telephone in any colour you liked as long as it was black!).

Without wishing to delve into the technology, an average UK domestic telephone set (or sets, as there are likely to be at least two in most homes) enables the customer to:

- choose a telephone provider of his or her choice, not necessarily British Telecom;
- have separate lines – most new properties are constructed with at least two telephone line connections;
- place extension sets throughout the house;

- see who is calling;
- receive answerphone messages;
- redial the last number automatically;
- see who was the last person to call;
- set up 'call waiting';
- divert calls;
- set up three-way calls;
- send and receive faxes;
- access the Internet and email using a modem and even using mobile phones.

The number of services increases almost monthly.

The earliest telegraphic connection between Europe and North America was laid by the Royal and US Navies and a later link was laid by the giant (for the time) steamship *Great Eastern* in the late 1860s. The development of telephone services was limited by wires until well after the Second World War. The 'space race' which led to the first moon landing in 1969, produced as a by-product the telecommunications satellite and freed the telephone from a total dependency on wires and thus made it possible to use many more channels.

The introduction of **ISDN** (Integrated Services Digital Network) in the 1990s has led to an explosion of telephone related services. Digital messages, unlike those sent by analogue means, allow the signal to be broken up into discrete packages. Thus a single wire can carry more than one 'conversation'. This allows computers (which use digital codes) to communicate very quickly as well as permitting much more complicated signals. Digital communications have made videoconferencing much more accessible as well as improving the quality of the vision and sound. ISDN gained rapid ground not only for business communications, where vast amounts of data need to be transmitted, but also in the home where a modem linked to an ISDN line could handle data much more quickly than a traditional analogue telephone system. ISDN is now giving way to **ADSL/broadband**, giving even greater access to the Internet.

As the number of home computers has grown, so has the requirement to access the Internet and email from home as well as at work, leading to the development of faster and faster modems and ISDN and later ADSL/Broadband, as covered above.

Telephones cannot be linked directly to the **CPU**. Initially the connection was via an acoustic cable. Today there is a **modem** (either internal or external) placed between the computer and the telephone line. Modern PCs come equipped with at least a 56 K modem.

Telnet

Telnet is terminal emulation that enables a user to connect to a remote host or device using a telnet client. Telnet enables a user to manage an account or device remotely. For example, a user may 'telnet' into a computer that hosts their website to remotely manage his or her files. Care needs to be taken to ensure that only authorized users can enter a system in this manner.

Template

Certain applications use template files to preload default configuration settings. Microsoft Word® uses a template called normal.dot to store information about page setup, margins and other document information.

Temporary files

A temporary file is a file created to hold information temporarily while a file is being created; they are in fact 'work in progress' files. After the program has been closed the temporary file can be deleted. Temporary files are used to help recover lost data if the program or computer is abnormally halted, as they can be opened and changed into permanent files.

Temporary Internet Files

Often referred to as the **cache**, the Temporary Internet Files folder contains a kind of record of the items a user has accessed, or downloaded from the web, including images, sounds, web pages and even **cookies**. Typically these items are stored in the Temporary Internet Files folder.

Storing these files in the cache can make browsing the web faster because it takes the computer less time to display a web page when it can call up some of the page's elements or even the entire page from the local Temporary Internet Files folder. This is especially useful if the page is one that is not updated regularly and can be viewed off-line.

All the files stored in the cache take up space, so from time to time the user needs to clear out the files stored in the cache to make more space available on the computer. This is known as 'clearing the cache' and can be accomplished very easily.

T

Text messaging

The ability to use mobile telephones to send alphanumeric messages. 'Texting', as it has become known, has been a fast-growing phenomenon, especially amongst young people. It is a very cost-effective means of sending a message when it is not necessary to speak to the other person, when multiple messages are required or when a copy of the message is needed. Text messaging is also useful when it is inconvenient for either the sender or the recipient to indulge in conversation. Text messaging is analogous to mobile **email**.

Thin film transistor (TTF)

A type of high-resolution **liquid crystal display (LCD)** often used in **laptops** and the LCD viewfinder in digital cameras and camcorders.

Time bomb

A malicious action (**virus**, **Trojan**) triggered at a specific date or time. Once a time bomb is on the hard disk of a computer it will sit there inactive until the computer's clock registers the time on which the bomb is set to go off. If the computer is up and running the bomb will activate. If the computer is not running the bomb may remain inactive. Many users refuse to use a computer on Friday 13th, as this date has been used by a number of time bombs.

Time-sharing

ICT systems in a commercial enterprise exist to support that enterprise. Such systems can be very expensive and thus need to operate at maximum capacity if money is not to be wasted and (for those organizations that are profit-making ones) the investment recouped. Time-sharing is the practice of allowing other users access to the system (with **firewall** protection of the organization's **data**).

Given the ease of data transmission today it is possible for a user in the UK to time-share a system in, say, India, where the time difference means that there may be periods when the Indian system is running at below capacity. Space on a computer can also be shared.

Toolbar

The toolbar is a set of boxes, often at the top and/or bottom of an application window, which control various functions of the software. The

Standard toolbar   Formatting toolbar

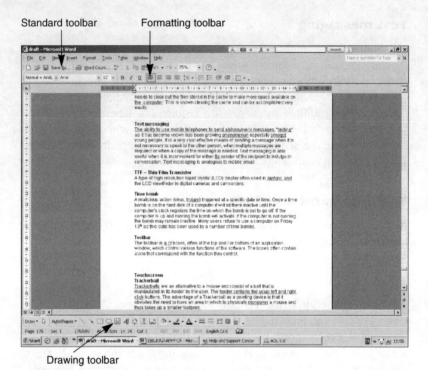

Drawing toolbar

Figure 44   Word® screen showing three toolbars

boxes often contain icons that correspond with the function they control (see Figure 44).

Touchscreen

A type of **monitor** with a sensitive panel directly on the screen that registers the touch of a finger or pen device as input. Some, instead of being touch-sensitive, use beams across the screen to create a grid which is interrupted by the presence of a finger or finger-like device near the screen. Touchscreens are popular for **PDAs** and as a **mouse** replacement on **laptop computers**. **Graphic tablets** employ similar pressure-sensitive technology. Touchscreens have also found ready application for giving out information in public places. They may be found on electronic directories in shopping complexes or in libraries etc. – anywhere that a casual user may need to access fairly specific information. A recent use has been for the issue of electronic boarding passes at airports. The traveller inputs his or her ticket details onto the touchscreen, confirms identity and then a boarding pass is issued.

Trackerball

Trackerballs are an alternative to a **mouse** and consist of a ball that is manipulated in its holder by the user. The holder contains the usual left and right click buttons. The advantage of a trackerball as a pointing device is that it obviates the need to have an area in which to physically manoeuvre a mouse and thus takes up a smaller **footprint**.

Transistors

A device composed of semiconductor material that amplifies a signal or opens or closes a circuit. Invented in 1947 at Bell Labs, transistors have become the key ingredient of all digital circuits, including computers. Today's microprocessors contain tens of millions of microscopic transistors.

Prior to the invention of transistors, digital circuits were composed of vacuum tubes, which had many disadvantages. They were much larger, required more energy, dissipated more heat, and were more prone to failures. It's safe to say that without the invention of transistors, computing as we know it today would not be possible.

Transputers

A transputer is the building block of a **parallel processing** system. Each transputer contains its own memory and processing elements plus a serial link to other transputers. By linking transputers together in a matrix a very powerful system can be built, as the addition of a transputer adds the full power of that transputer to the system. One of the problems that still requires a complete solution is how to split the processing problem up into separate parts for each transputer to handle.

Trojan

A trojan is a malicious program that pretends to be a benign application; a trojan horse program purposefully does something the user does not expect or know about. Trojans are not viruses since they do not replicate, but can be just as destructive because they disrupt computer use and may wipe out files etc.

T

Ultra-Large Scale Integration (ULSI)

An **integrated circuit** with more than one million components per chip.

See also **Large Scale Integration** and **Very Large Scale Integration (VLSI)**.

UNIX

UNIX is a multi-user, multi-tasking operating system developed at Bell Labs in the early 1970s.

UNIX was one of the first operating systems to be written in a high-level programming language, known as C, in the case of UNIX. This enabled UNIX to be installed on virtually any computer for which a C compiler existed. This natural portability, combined with its low price, made it a popular choice among universities. (It was inexpensive because the US government's anti-trust regulations prohibited Bell Labs from marketing it as a full-scale product.)

Bell Labs distributed the operating system in its source language form, so anyone who obtained a copy could modify and customize it for his own purposes. By the end of the 1970s, dozens of different versions of UNIX were running at various sites.

Due to its portability, flexibility and power, UNIX has become a leading operating system for workstations, although it has been less popular in the personal computer market.

Unzip

The opening up of a compressed file.

See **zip**.

Upload

The process of taking a file (text, photo, video, sound etc.) from the computer and sending it to a server on the Internet (perhaps as an **email** attachment). The use of **ADSL/Broadband** has made the process of uploading large files much quicker as these systems can reduce the time required by a factor of between 10 and 20. **Downloading** is the process of sending a file from a **server** on the **Internet** to the computer.

URL (Uniform Resource Locator)

As generally used the URL for a page is that page's Internet address.

URLs are similar to the type of address we have for our homes and businesses and are unique to a particular page. Once you have the URL for a page you can direct the web **browser** to it.

For example, if we look at the different elements in the address http://www.palgrave.com/resources/index.asp

- http://

  The http:// stands for Hypertext Transfer Protocol and is the system used on the Internet to transfer web pages.

  If a site is secure the prefix will be https://

  http:// tells the browser to look for a web page, https:// tells the browser to look for a secure web page. Other prefixes include:

ftp:// (	
news (note no ://)	this is a **newsgroup** address
gopher://	an early means of web navigation
mailto:	opens the email system telenet:// (similar to **gopher**)

- www.

  The www indicates that the page is on the **World Wide Web**.

- palgrave.com

  This is the **domain name**.

- resources/index

  This indicates where the particular page resides on the Palgrave website.

- .asp

  This indicates an Active Server Page **(ASP)**.

U

USB (Universal Serial Bus)

An external **bus** developed by Intel, Compaq, DEC, IBM, Microsoft, NEC and Northern Telecom and released to the public in 1996 with the Intel 430HX Triton II **motherboard**. USB has the capability of supporting a number of devices at one time.

If a computer supports USB the symbol shown in Figure 45 will be found on it.

USB cables are hot-swappable, which means that users can connect and disconnect the cable while the computer is on without any physical damage to the cable. Figures 46 and 47 show what the end of a USB connector looks like. There are two standards of USB connectors. Type A connectors are found on the computer and/or USB hub and Type B

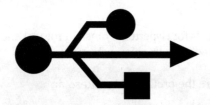

Figure 45 USB symbol

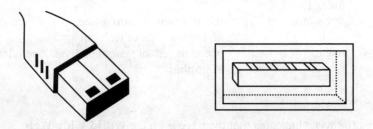

Figure 46 Type A USB connector and slot (computer)

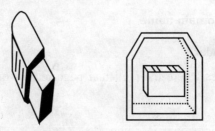

Figure 47 Type B USB connector and slot (device)

connectors are found on the peripheral. USB cables should legally be only 5m (16 ft) maximum as defined by the USB standard. When exceeding this length or utilizing extensions in the cables, data loss will occur.

The ability of USB to support the use of multiple devices with relative ease has led to the development of a whole series of USB products, for example:

Cameras – USB cameras are available for fast transfer of data.

CD-ROM drives – External USB CD-ROM drives are available for quick data transfers.

Converters – USB converters are now available to enable old serial, parallel, SCSI and PS/2 devices to be used.

Joysticks – Joysticks and other gaming devices are available for fast and quick connections.

Keyboards

Microphones

Modems – USB modems are now an available option.

Monitors

Mouses – USB mouses are now available and generally provide a smoother connection than the PS/2 port.

MP3 players – Portable MP3 players can now connect via the USB port to transfer data.

Network – Network options are available to connect to networks utilizing the USB port.

Printers

Removable media – Various types of USB removable media are available, such as tape drives, floppy, zip, super disk and many more.

Scanners – Various types of scanners are available through USB for fast and easy connectivity.

Speakers – USB speakers are now available with various new options.

TV tuners – USB TV tuners are now available for users to have the availability of watching TV via the USB port.

See also **USB hub**.

USB hub

A peripheral device that is plugged into a **USB** socket of the computer and which has a number of separate USB sockets of its own, thus expanding the number of USB devices that can be used. The USB hub may operate using the host computer's power supply or may need a separate supply of its own. USB hubs have made the task of expanding the number of ports that the system possesses very easy and inexpensive as it is literally just a question of plugging the hub into one of the system's USB ports; there is a four (or more)-fold increase in the number of USB ports and thus also in the number of USB-enabled devices that can be left plugged into the system.

U

VDU (Visual Display Unit)

See monitors.

Very-Large Scale Integration (VLSI)

An integrated circuit design that contains 5000 to 50,000 components on a single chip.

See also **Large Scale Integration** and **Ultra-Large Scale Integration (ULSI)**.

VGA (Video Graphics Array)

VGA is a popular display standard developed by IBM and introduced in 1987. VGA provides either for 640 × 480 resolution colour display screens with a refreshment rate of 60 Hz and 16 colours displayed at a time, or, if the resolution is lowered to 320 × 200, 256 colours can be displayed. VGA capability is built into **plug-in video cards**, VGA chips, and monitors that can work with the VGA cards. VGA has now been largely replaced by **SVGA**.

Videoconferencing

The successor to **teleconferencing**, videoconferencing uses **Broadband** and **web cams** to link participants for a meeting or seminar regardless of their global location.

Given the importance of face-to-face contact, including an ability to use body language to gain clues about real thinking, it is not surprising that the use of the Internet is at an early stage when it comes to managing people. It is doubtful whether any court or tribunal would look kindly upon the hiring, and especially firing of staff purely by email at the moment.

There are organizations, however, where the staff are so widely scattered that the sheer geography of the situation makes the use of electronic communications not just useful but a key part of the organization's ability to function and survive.

Virtuality (e.g. virtual university, virtual shop etc.)

Organizations that operate with little in the way of premises, relying on the Internet to communicate with their customers. A virtual shop may be nothing more than a **workstation** in a house with orders being sent to a wholesaler who then delivers to the customer. **E-commerce** has led to a huge growth in organizations that have few premises but a huge customer base.

Virus

A computer program file capable of attaching to disks or other files and replicating itself repeatedly, typically without user knowledge or permission. Some viruses attach to files so that when the infected file executes, the virus also executes. Other viruses sit in a computer's memory and infect files as the computer opens, modifies or creates the files. Some viruses display symptoms, and some viruses damage files and computer systems, but neither symptoms nor damage is essential in the definition of a virus; a non-damaging virus is still a virus.

> See also **Trojan**.

Virus checkers

Virus checkers are software applications that scan the computer's drives for any **viruses** etc. and then inform the user. The more advanced checkers (often known as **anti-virus software**) can also take action to remedy the situation by quarantining the infected file. Virus checkers can also scan Internet content and emails and advise the user before the virus has an opportunity to enter the system. This form of permanent protection runs in the background all the time the computer is switched on. As viruses have proliferated, so many **Internet Service Providers (ISPs)** have provided automatic scanning of emails as part of their service. By the end of May 2004, Panda – one of the leading anti-virus software providers, together with Norton and McAfree – had over 78,000 listed viruses that the software could deal with.

V

Virus checkers are only effective if updated on a regular basis. Panda updates automatically on connecting to the **Internet**. Regular scans of the system should be carried out to check that no viruses have got through the protection.

Virus remedies

The first remedy is for the user to be very careful about opening email attachments and to be selective about which **Internet** sites are viewed. A serious attack may require the whole system to be reloaded onto the computer. Where a virus is detected by **anti-virus software** the offending file is quarantined and a repair attempted. If the repair fails the file can be deleted from quarantine.

Voice recognition software

Software applications that can recognize the voice of the user, who can then input commands using a microphone rather than keyboard and mouse. Such systems need to be taught to recognize the accent and nuances of the user and are thus user-specific. The more they are used, the more efficient they become due to their ability to learn. Voice-activated software not only inputs text but can also operate computer commands. This makes it ideal for those with disabilities.

Volatile

A volatile memory is one that loses its data when the power is switched off (cf. **Bubble memory**).

WWW (World Wide Web)

The term World Wide Web (WWW) refers to all of the publicly accessible websites in the world, in addition to other information sources that web browsers can access. These other sources include FTP sites, Usenet newsgroups, and the few remaining Gopher sites.

The World Wide Web was invented by Tim Berners-Lee, in 1990, while working at CERN (the European Organization for Nuclear Research). He went on to found the World Wide Web Consortium, which seeks to standardize and improve World Wide Web-related things, such as the Hypertext Markup Language (HTML) in which web pages are written. Specifically, Tim Berners-Lee wrote the first web browser and the first web server. He invented both the original HTML and the HTTP (Hypertext Transfer Protocol) used to request and transmit web pages between web servers and web browsers. He christened his developments 'The World Wide Web'.

The World Wide Web is not the Internet, although it does form a very important part of it. Sites that are part of the World Wide Web have the prefix www.

WAN (Wide Area Network)

A computer network that uses ICT to link users over a wide geographic area (cf. LAN). Such networks are often connected using dedicated cabling or telephone lines. Within each site there may be a more self-contained **Local Area Network (LAN)** using its own server, each **server** being then connected to the WAN server. Because of the dispersed nature of a WAN the configuration is likely to be that of a star network, as described in the Local Area Network (LAN) section. An example of an early WAN in the UK is described below.

During the mid-1980s, in response to a series of government initiatives and legislation, the UK local authority of Kent County Council reorganized the administration of the education service within the county. Kent was one of the largest UK authorities, with a budget that approached that of a small nation. In order to give maximum autonomy on operational issues to local managers while retaining central policy control (in accordance with the ideas of Peters and Waterman, 2004) it was decided to set up a series of area offices that would have a management function and would replace a larger number of mainly administrative district offices.

Kent is a large county and it was realized that effective communication, including that of data and documents, would be vital to the success of the proposal. Area offices (each itself the size of the education department in many urban boroughs) were set up around the county as shown in Figure 48. The HQ of the education service remained at the Springfield site located just outside the county town, Maidstone.

To facilitate communication the County Council installed one of the UK's first non-military WANs using equipment provided by Data General. For many employees this was their first experience of **email**. By using dedicated British Telecom telephone lines it was possible to link the area offices with HQ (and through HQ with each other) and to establish a fast and effective means of sending messages and documents

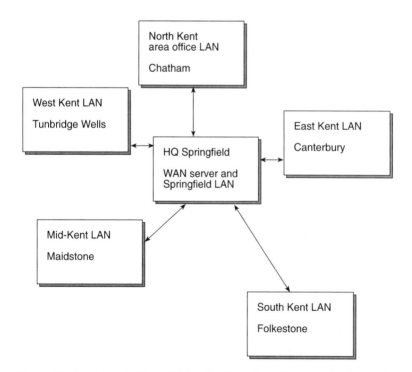

Figure 48   Kent County Council Education Department's reorganization in the 1980s

around the county. The use of dedicated lines, while incurring leasing costs, meant that there were no actual call costs and this proved to present considerable value for money. So successful (and innovative) was this approach, that the organization received not only visitors from other UK authorities and commercial organizations but also interest from abroad. This initiative was one of the earliest non-military applications of the new possibilities of ICT in the UK.

Peters, T. and Waterman, R. (1982), *In Search of Excellence*, 2nd edn (Profile Business).

Regan, P. (2003), *Wide Area Networks* (Eaglewood Cliffs, NJ: Prentice Hall).

WAP (Wireless Application Protocol)

WAP is the specifications for a set of communication protocols used to allow wireless devices to access the Internet and other network utilities such as email, chat, etc. WAP-enabled mobile phones are now in regular use and allow the user not only to speak on the telephone but also to send picture files etc. To accomplish this a small **digital camera** is included as part of the handset. Such telephones allow a user to access his or her **Internet Service Provider** and through the ISP collect **email** and access the **Internet**.

Web authoring software

A category of software that enables the user to develop a **website** in a **desktop publishing (DTP)** format. The software will generate the required **HTML** coding for the layout of the web pages based on what the user designs. Typically, the user can toggle back and forth between the graphical design and the HTML code and make changes to the web page in either the design or the accompanying code. The advent of such software has made website design that much easier for those who have no technical skills although they still need to consider the marketing aspects of any design.

Web directories

Unlike **search engines** (i.e. **programs** that search through **Internet** sites) web directories are search aids that are compiled by real people who then ensure that the directories are kept up to date. Most search engines also have associated directories provided to enhance the service offered and thus encourage use of that particular search engine. Yahoo!, Altavista, Excite, Google etc. all have directories.

The following examples of how a directory works are taken from the

May 2004 directories offered by the main Yahoo! site. In addition to its main site, Yahoo! provides directories for:

North and South America
Argentina, Brazil, Canada, Mexico (Chinese and Spanish offered in the USA)

Europe
Catalan speakers, Denmark, France, Germany, Italy, Norway, Spain, Sweden, UK and Eire

Asia
Australia and New Zealand, China, Hong Kong (separate directory to China), India, Japan, Korea, Singapore, Taiwan

There are also dedicated pages for major US cities.

Each directory is subdivided (see Figure 49). For example, the 'Society and culture' directory on the main site is divided into 'People', 'Environment' and 'Religion'. The People sub-directory is then divided

Figure 49 The Yahoo! directories
Reproduced with permission of Yahoo! Inc. YAHOO! and the YAHOO! logo are trademarks of Yahoo! Inc.

into categories, e.g. under 'C' these are: 'Celebrities', 'Chefs', 'Comedians' and 'Computer and Internet'. Within each category will be found details of the people the compilers feel should be included.

Directories are extremely useful if the user knows exactly what he or she wants. They are especially useful in e-commerce as they can list organizations by product/service and geographic location.

The disadvantage of web directories is the same as paper-based versions: the user is dependent upon the person compiling the directory. Unlike a web search, where all the sites that fit the search criteria can be found, a directory only lists those chosen by its compilers.

Web host

These are companies that store and serve websites for others. The services they offer include:

- design of site;
- updating of site;
- **domain name** registration;
- tracking and compilation of statistics on visits to the site;
- registering with **search engines**.

The use of a web host means that even the smallest business is able to have a website and offer links to other sites, sell merchandise etc. without the capital outlay on systems or the need for expertise in website design. Many hosting companies provide a design service for their clients.

Web server

A web server is one that is dedicated to store and host Internet sites. Large organizations may have their website served by their own system, while smaller users may employ the services of a **web host** company.

Webcam

A small camera, usually attached to the top of the computer **monitor** or **screen**, that allows video footage to be sent via the Internet in real time. Webcam definition is improving all the time thanks to the increasing use of **Broadband**. Webcam technology is also employed in many new generation mobile telephones to allow images to be sent to and from them.

Webcams have brought the dream of video-telecommunications as an everyday part of life that much closer. Far from being expensive, they are very cheap indeed. America On Line gave away free webcams to those signing up for its Broadband services in 2004.

Website

A central location of various web pages that are all related and can be accessed by visiting the homepage. The vast majority of websites contain **hypertext links** that direct the user either to different pages within the site or to another site altogether.

Such has been the growth of the Internet that there are now very few small and medium-sized business that do not have a website. Almost every branch of government, be it local, national or supra-national (like the European Union), has a website as (at the opposite end of the scale) do a growing number of individuals.

Website designer

An individual whose area of expertise is the design of websites. Website design is a growing area. Those involved need a blend of marketing skills and ICT knowledge. A website is more than just advertising; much of its strength lies in its **hypertext links**.

See also **web host**.

WiFi (Wireless Fidelity)

WiFi utilizes agreed standards to achieve a wireless network. A home wireless network commonly broadcasts a signal using a WAP to send and receive signals from wireless devices on the network.

WIMP (Windows, Icon, Menus, Pointer)

It is the user-friendly nature of WIMP that has made the whole Windows® concept so all-pervading. Using WIMP a newcomer to computers is able to get up and running with tasks in a reasonably short period of time. WIMP has transformed the computer elements of **Information and Communication Technology (ICT)** from a specialist area to one where the average person can run an application with only minimal training (Figure 50 shows WIMP in Word®).

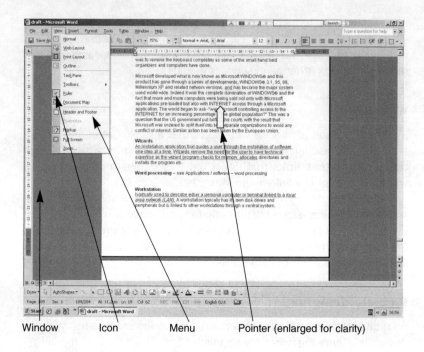

Window   Icon   Menu   Pointer (enlarged for clarity)

Figure 50   WIMP

Windows®

Apple computers were the first to offer an operating environment that used a mouse and icons to point and click rather than keyboard inputs. Indeed one idea was to remove the keyboard completely – as indeed some of the small hand-held organizers and computers have done.

Microsoft developed what is now known as Microsoft Windows® and this product has gone through a series of developments – Windows® 3.1, 95, 98, Millennium XP and related network versions – and has become the major system used worldwide. Indeed, it was the complete domination of Windows® (and the fact that more and more computers were being sold not only with Microsoft applications preloaded but also with Internet access through a Microsoft application) that made the world begin to ask whether Microsoft was controlling access to the Internet for an increasing percentage of the global population. This was a question that the US government put before the courts, with the result that Microsoft was ordered to split itself into two separate organizations to avoid any conflict of interest. Similar action has been taken by the European Union.

Microsoft Windows® has undergone considerable transformation over the years as extra functionality has been added. A huge range and quantity of software applications are available and this has further helped increase its market dominance. With a complete range of versions for both home and network use, the Microsoft concept of Windows® has achieved global dominance.

Wingdings

Wingdings are **Microsoft** fonts designed by Kris Holmes and Charles Bigelow in 1990 and 1991. The three font sets provide a harmoniously designed set of icons representing the common components of personal computer systems and the elements of graphical user interfaces. There are icons for PC, monitor, keyboard, mouse, trackerball, hard drive, diskette, tape cassette, printer, fax, etc., as well as icons for file folders, documents, mail, mailboxes, windows, clipboard and wastebasket. In addition, Wingdings includes icons with both traditional and computer significance, such as writing tools and hands, reading glasses, clipping scissors, bell, bomb, check boxes, as well as more traditional images such as weather signs, religious symbols, astrological signs, encircled numerals, a selection of ampersands and interrobangs, plus elegant flowers and flourishes. Pointing and indicating are frequent functions in graphical interfaces, so in addition to a wide selection of pointing hands, the Wingdings fonts also offer arrows in careful gradations of weight and different directions and styles. For variety and impact as bullets, asterisks and ornaments, Wingdings also offers a varied set of geometric circles, squares, polygons, targets and stars.

Windings provide the Microsoft user with an easy way to import simple graphical and iconic representations into documents (see Figure 51 for examples).

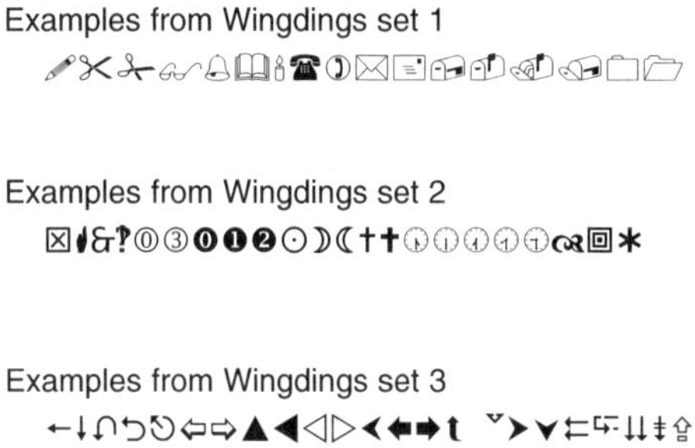

Examples from Wingdings set 1

✏✂✁✁✁▣✆☎①✉✉📂📂🗐🗁

Examples from Wingdings set 2

⊠✐✇✆①③❶❷❸⓪)(✝✝①①①①①◐◐✳

Examples from Wingdings set 3

←↓∩↺↻⇦⇨▲◀◁▷◀↩➡↑ ˅➤Y⟾⟾⇊‡☖

Figure 51 Wingdings

Wizards

Applications that guide a user through the installation of software one step at a time. Wizards remove the need for the user to have technical expertise because the wizard program checks for memory, allocates directories and installs the program etc. The use of wizards has made installing new software an extremely easy task. The user does not have to create directories or worry about the installation process. Wizards ask simple user-friendly questions that normally require only a YES, NO or NEXT response from the user. Once the installation has been completed most wizards even restart the computer to complete the process. Wizards are also used to guide users through an application, e.g. setting up a spreadsheet.

Word processing

See **applications/software – word processing.**

Workstation

Normally used to describe either a personal computer or terminal linked to a **local area network (LAN)**. A workstation typically has its own disk drives and peripherals but is linked to other workstations through a central system.

Effective workstation design involves a consideration of **ergonomics** to ensure that the health and safety of the user is protected and that he or she can work as efficiently as possible.

Firstly, the system should rest on an antistatic mat. The discharge of static electricity can (in exceptional circumstances) injure a person and can also damage components. The height of the workstation needs to be considered: is it adjustable? The norm for workstation height is 710 mm, which might not suit a short or tall person. Chair design needs consideration – back problems lose UK industry many, many days per year. Cathode ray **monitors** need anti-glare screens to protect the user from eye fatigue. The lighting in the area needs to be optimized. Wrists need to be protected from **repetitive strain injury (RSI)** by the use of special pads that fit in front of the keyboard and provide additional support to the muscles.

The placement of peripherals and documentation should be such as to avoid the need for excessive twisting movements. The development of flat screens (see TFT) has increased the **footprint** available for peripherals although 'Parkinson's Law' suggests that the space saved will soon be overflowing with new devices!

World Wide Web (WWW)

See **WWW** – p. 192.

Worm

Worms are parasitic computer programs that replicate but, unlike **viruses**, do not infect other computer program files. Worms can create copies on the same computer, or can send the copies to other computers via a network. Worms can spread via IRC (Internet Relay Chat), email or by establishing a direct connection to the target computer. Although they do not infect files, by replicating worms can rapidly use up memory and also network bandwith.

WYSIWYG ('What You See Is What You Get')

When a user looks at the screen while running a program such as a **spreadsheet**, **word processor** or **desktop publisher** on a modern computer he or she can be fairly sure that what will be printed is exactly what appears on the screen. Early versions of such software also contained commands on the screen, none of which would be printed out unless requested. In many ways it was this inability to provide a WYSIWYG ('What You See Is What You Get') environment that put many potential users off computers, as it seemed as if it was necessary to learn all the commands (as indeed it was with some early programs). The advent of **WIMP** (Windows, Icon, Menus and Pointer) changed all that and now users can concentrate on the application and have an easy method of laying out and printing text etc.

XML (eXtensible Markup Language)

XML is similar to **HTML** in that it uses tags to mark-up a document, allowing a browser to interpret the tags and display them on a page. However, unlike HTML, XML language is unlimited and allows self-defining tags.

Zip

Zip archive file. A zip archive contains compressed collections of other files. Zip files are popular on the Internet because users can deliver multiple files in a single container; the compressed files also save disk space and download time. Zip is also used as a brand name by **Iomega** for a magnetic media high-memory storage device that is relatively easy to read and write to.

Zip files need a special program such as **Unzip** in order for them to be read.

Relevant Websites

www.amazon.com	Amazon.com main website
www.amazon.co.uk	Amazon UK website
www.aol.com	America On Line website
www.belkin.com	Belkin website
www.canon.com	Canon website
www.compaq.com	Compaq website
www.computerhope.com	Computing definitions website
www.dell.com	Dell website
www.google.com	Google website
www.hp.com	Hewlett Packard (HP) website
www.ibm.com	IBM website
www.intel.com	Intel Corporation website
www.iomega.com	Iomega website
www.metacrawler.com	Metacrawler search agent website
www.microsoft.com	Microsoft website
www.mp3sound.com	Information about mp3
www.packardbell.com	Packard Bell website
www.sharp.co.uk	Sharp website
www.sun.com	Sun Microsystems website
www.supernews.com	Newsgroup information
http://tile.net (note no www.)	Tile website
www.toshiba.com	Toshiba website
www.uhi.ac.uk	University of the Highlands and Islands Millennium Institute website
www.w3c.org	World Wide Web Consortium website
www.yahoo.com	Yahoo website

Index